marvelous
motherhood

marvelous motherhood

the essential guide to
looking and feeling great after pregnancy

Jo Glanville-Blackburn

with photography by Dan Duchars

RYLAND
PETERS
& SMALL

LONDON NEW YORK

To my late mother, Margaret Patricia Glanville-Blackburn, who used to sneak me out of school every so often so we could go shopping. Great fun, Mom!

DESIGNER Sonya Nathoo
SENIOR EDITOR Henrietta Heald
PICTURE RESEARCH Tracy Ogino
PRODUCTION Patricia Harrington
ART DIRECTOR Gabriella Le Grazie
PUBLISHING DIRECTOR Alison Starling

ILLUSTRATIONS Javier Joaquin

First published in the USA in 2005 by
Ryland Peters & Small
519 Broadway
5th Floor
New York, NY 10012
www.rylandpeters.com
10 9 8 7 6 5 4 3 2 1

Library of Congress Cataloging-in-Publication Data

Glanville-Blackburn, Jo.
  Marvelous motherhood : the essential guide to looking and
great after pregnancy / Jo Glanville-Blackburn with photography by
Dan Duchars.
      p. cm.
  Includes index.
  ISBN 1-84172-838-1
1. Postnatal care–Popular works. 2. Mothers–Health and hygiene–
Popular works. 3. Mothers–Nutrition–Popular works. 4. Beauty,
Personal. I. Title.
  RG801.G56 2005
  618.2–dc22
                                    2004026564

Printed and bound in China.

Neither the author nor the publisher can be held responsible
for any claim arising out of the use or misuse of suggestions
made in this book. While every effort has been made to
ensure that the information contained in the book is accurate
and up to date, it is advisory only and should not be used as
an alternative to seeking specialized medical advice.

contents

introduction

One of the many wise sayings about motherhood is that it takes nine months to make a baby and another nine months to get over it. And get over it we do—with a little time. Otherwise, none of us would feel the need or desire to do it again, would we?

Regardless of how "good" your birth experience was, nothing quite prepares you for the few weeks following it. Some women (and men, too, I should add) sail through the postpartum period—those first six weeks when everything is so different from what it was before—but most of us, if we are honest about it, end up feeling helpless and confused, even a bit desperate, from time to time.

While writing this book, I consulted a mind and body therapist who is also a mother of two, hoping that she would divulge lots of useful tips. Instead, she gave me a grimace and said, "Babies! They leave you in a state of unknown. You don't know anything. You don't know who you are. You question your whole identity. It does bad things to your body . . ." Well, let's just say she went on a bit.

For a moment or two, it threw me. Was I really trying to make out that there was anything positive about the aftershock of pregnancy? But then, of course, there is—something more positive than words can describe. There it is in your arms, offering you every reason for trying to look and feel as positive as you can—without denying the times when it is a struggle and you need help. Everything that happens to

you in the hours, days, and weeks after the birth has a knock-on effect on your happiness and contentment—and on the wellbeing and development of your baby. Which means that there is definitely place for this book—so I went ahead and wrote it anyway.

Right now you are probably on a bigger emotional rollercoaster than you are likely to experience at any other time in your life. Those hormones that played havoc with your mind and body while you were pregnant are still at it. You have given birth to the baby, and levels of oestrogen and progesterone in your body, which rose to very high levels at the birth, are trying hard to settle down, but they can of course end up plummeting, throwing every emotional and physical possibility in your path.

You may have had nine months to prepare you for this moment—being in your home with your new baby—and yet you are bound to have occasional feelings of doubt and panic about the whole thing. The sudden realization comes upon you that there is now someone very small who is completely dependent upon you all the time for love, devotion, and support.

And that little baby is now everything to you, too—which is why I think you will find this book useful. For, in becoming a mother, you must never lose sight of yourself. *Marvelous Motherhood* is written entirely for you and about you, the new mother. Right now, from the very first day, you need to seek a new balance in your life and try to look after yourself—to demonstrate that you value your own individuality, rather than becoming lost in the identity of "Mom." The most valuable lesson I learned as a new parent—three times over—was to let go of life a little. I had to remind myself not to expect everything to be as perfect as it seems in movies and magazines (which, believe me, after many years spent in the industry was hard). Real life simply isn't like that.

I hope that your experience of new motherhood is a time of joy and fulfillment. Cherish ever part of your babe: the nape of the neck, the curve and dimple of the elbow, the poreless delicate beauty of the skin. Such perfection is so transient in life. As many other people around you will say, "Make the most of this time—they grow up so fast." And they do. So relish this brief moment. It will be gone before you know it. For in the space of this first year, you will not believe the changes that take place—to your baby and to yourself.

Being a mother has been, and remains, the most blissful experience of my life. Although my children have now reached the ages of nine, seven, and three—and frequently push their parents to the brink of patience and beyond—it is that unconditional "I will love you above everything" passion that remains so remarkable and so thrilling.

JO GLANVILLE-BLACKBURN

the new you

Your life has changed forever. From now on, you will be defined less as an individual and more as a mother. There will be choices ahead—many joyous, a few difficult—but you have embarked on an exciting journey called motherhood, and as it progresses, you will discover many, often unexpected, things about yourself.

the first few hours

How are you feeling? Exhausted? Elated? Full of wonder at the small person you have brought into the world? This is, indeed, a moment to treasure. You may feel that you would be happy to gaze at this new being forever—and that your love will grow, unconditionally.

IMMEDIATELY AFTER THE BIRTH

It is quite normal to feel excited, tired, and amazed all at once in the first few hours after delivery. You may also experience a wonderful sense of calm and relief. You will be able to hold, look at, and talk to your baby. During the first hour or so after the birth, you can also expect to introduce your baby to feeding from the breast (if you are planning to breastfeed).

What you are unlikely to do, however, is sleep—no matter how tired you may be. It could be rapture that keeps you awake. It could be nerves: "I daren't close my eyes in case something happens," or "What do I do now?" All kinds of thoughts will race through your mind. At a time when your baby is more than likely to need rest after the ordeal of birth, you will probably feel the most awake and alert you have felt for a while.

This period of wakefulness seems to be essential to allow new mothers to come to terms with the enormity of the life changes that have taken place. What few people tell you in advance is that from this moment on, you will be on "mommy alert," meaning that you will probably never sleep deeply again—at least until long after your child has started school.

"I shall never forget that first night," a close friend of mine confided. "I never slept. I just gazed at my beloved little girl, resting and suckling away. Needless to say, I was exhausted, but nothing will ever erase that blissful first moment of deep adoration and love." Capture all the positive emotions of your birth experience and treasure the memory of them—they will help you to cope better over the next few months.

DELIVERY OF THE PLACENTA

Within half an hour of the birth, the placenta detaches and passes out of the uterus through the vagina. This is regarded as the third stage of labor. You may be given oxytocin to help the process. Contractions will continue until after the placenta is delivered, so you may have to concentrate and breathe through this uncomfortable stage—or you may be so involved with your new baby that you hardly notice the delivery of the placenta.

YOUR PHYSICAL HEALTH

During the first hours after birth, a health professional will carry out the following checks and procedures.
□ Repair your perineum if you have had a tear or an episiotomy.
□ Remove the small tube in your back (called an epidural catheter) if you had epidural anesthesia. Your legs may feel numb for up to six hours afterward, and you may experience tingling or shaking of the legs.
□ Massage your uterus by rubbing your lower abdomen about every 15 minutes. This will help it to contract, or tighten, and reduce bleeding. If your uterus does not contract, it may bleed too much. Later, you may be taught how to massage your own uterus.

"As I watched my seven-year-old son, William, sleeping the other night, curled up in his bed, I was instantly taken back to our first night together—a moment I shall never forget."

JO, MOTHER OF OLIVIA, WILLIAM, AND PHOEBE

□ Check your bladder to make sure it is not full. A full bladder puts pressure on your uterus, which interferes with contractions. You will be asked to try to urinate, which may be difficult because of pain and swelling. If you cannot urinate, a catheter can be used to empty the bladder. A urination problem usually passes quickly.

□ Check your blood pressure at regular intervals over a period of several hours.

COMING DOWN TO EARTH

If you have given birth at home, you can eat and drink whatever you like; if you are in the hospital, however, food and drink (unless supplied by your partner) will be limited. Eat what you can for energy. You won't be in the hospital long. Unless you have had a cesarean (in which case, you will probably stay in for four to five days), you may be discharged within a few hours if there were no complications.

Sooner or later, you will become more aware of how you and your body feel. Unless you are prepared for it, the reality of the early postpartum period can be quite a shock to a new mother. Not only are you and your tiny baby no longer one complete unit, but also you are sore, uncomfortable and perhaps leaking milk, urine, and blood all at once. I am sorry to start off on such a negative note—but that is sometimes the way it is.

A TIME TO REJOICE

As long as you receive enough emotional and practical support, you should discover that, despite the physical upheaval, the postpartum period really can be a joyous time. Fortunately, there is much you can do to make the rough patches a bit smoother. My advice is to try not to get worked up about anything. With nature's help you will cope admirably—especially if you let your body rest, recover and "do its thing." Getting used to having a baby is an entirely new experience. You may feel that you have bonded instantly—that you have known this child inside you for nine months and that now you are simply adjusting to a new stage of the relationship. Equally, you may not feel that way at all. Many new mothers berate themselves for not falling head over heels in love with their babies. Babies need attention—lots of it. You are the one who has had most of the attention for the past nine months, and now the baby is getting it all. There are many ways to rationalize your feelings. I say discuss them. Talking helps to put things into perspective—so don't bottle up your emotions.

BACK AT HOME

Well in advance of your baby's birth (ideally), stock up on essential "emergency" provisions such as canned foods, soups, soft toilet paper, and toothpaste. If you have the inclination and the freezer space, double the quantities of your recipes when you cook dinner and freeze half for later.

If you have older children, write down a list of their schedules. It is hard enough to keep track of your own life with a new baby, let alone that of the rest of the family. Simply make a calendar for the week so you will know who has ballet or football practice and when. This will also allow someone else (such as your partner) to help without having to ask you all the time.

Visits to your home by family and friends can be a lot of fun, but they can also be very draining in the early days. Leave an answering-machine message giving the details about the birth that you would like known and a short message about when you will be happy to

although you may feel **disoriented** by what you have **been** through, this period can be a time of **great joy** receive visitors. Signs on the door can be useful, too. Many hospitals provide them automatically—why not try the same tactic at home? A straightforward "Mother and baby sleeping" is usually very effective.

BABY AND MOTHER CHECKLISTS

Necessary items for your baby include diapers, cotton balls, and diaper rash cream (I always used chamomile ointment, which most of the time healed a sore bottom by the next diaper change—as well as soothing sore nipples). You will also need three cotton blankets, three undersheets, and several gauze squares. Undershirts and snuggle suits are the most practical clothes for tiny babies and the easiest to change. Firstborns are often "dressed up," but consider what is most convenient for you and comfortable for your baby.

For yourself, you will need a good supply of maxi maternity pads, breast pads (the kind that use diaper silicone technology, keeping your nipples dry even when they are soaked), a soothing body oil or cream to keep your now slack tummy supple and hydrated, and a good hand cream that doesn't leave your palms greasy.

a happy mother means a happy baby

No matter how well you prepare for it, having a new baby to love and care for is a challenge, but making your own life simpler in the period after the birth will boost your confidence and help minimize any negative feelings—a wonderful start to positive parenting.

ALL ABOUT YOU

Make time and space to look after yourself and be a little self-indulgent. Showering or soaking in a bath at least once a day and washing your hair will make you feel better and give you a few minutes of solitude.

REDUCE SOURCES OF STRESS

Having someone around to help for the first few weeks after the birth can be a real blessing. It may be your husband, a friend, a relative, or even a professional, such as a maternity nurse. The key thing is that it should be someone who will empower you and your partner as new parents rather than doing everything for you.

Write down a list of things that need to be done and never turn down offers of help from friends—give them options to choose from, such as doing a load of laundry or bringing you a meal. Ask your baby's father to help whenever possible. He is just as capable of changing a diaper, burping, or bathing the baby as you are. The only thing he cannot do is breastfeed.

SLEEP

It is essential to follow the advice to "sleep when the baby sleeps." Many new mothers are tempted to skip a few minutes of nap time to do chores—but these can wait or be done by your friends or partner. Accept that you cannot cope with everything and there is no need to create the impression of managing and multitasking brilliantly. If you don't get enough rest, in a few weeks' time you may be producing insufficient milk for your baby as well as feeling depressed and exhausted.

WARNING SIGNS

One sign that you are overdoing things is an increase in the vaginal blood flow that continues for several weeks after childbirth (the lochia) or a change in the color of the flow to bright red. Here are some warning signs to be alert for in the postpartum period. If you have any of the following symptoms, consult your doctor:

□ A temperature higher than 101°F (38°C).

□ Severe pain, redness, or swelling at the episiotomy or cesarean incision.

□ A smelly vaginal discharge.

□ Heavy blood flow that soaks more than one maxi pad in an hour.

□ A red, tender spot on one breast (which may have a lump under it).

□ Crying that lasts for days.

□ Suicidal thoughts.

□ Thoughts of harming the baby.

banishing the blues

The rollercoaster of motherhood will make your moods rise and fall on a daily basis. Your success in coping with the challenges that you will surely meet depends to a large extent on how well you look after yourself at this time.

THE PHYSICAL YOU

During pregnancy, the levels of particular hormones in the mother's body rise to create the right environment for the growing fetus. In the postpartum period the body experiences further dramatic changes in hormone levels, which begin at the onset of labor.

Within 24 hours of the birth, the progesterone and estrogen in the body often sink to a lower level than before conception. The physical strain from this sudden drop is intensified by the complex changes that take place in the body to prepare for milk production.

THE EMOTIONAL YOU

It will come as no surprise to learn that, with all these physical changes going on in the new mother, there will be psychological changes as well. Every woman experiences these in a different way. Some women have no negative feelings at all after childbirth; others have adverse reactions ranging through the spectrum from mild to moderate to severe. The mildest form of the condition is often referred to as the "baby blues" and affects the largest proportion of new mothers. The

moderate form is known as postpartum depression; the severest form is postpartum psychosis—a disease that is still the subject of extensive research.

Regardless of how prepared you might have been for the period after birth, the responsibility and demands of caring for a tiny new life 24 hours a day, seven days a week—not to mention anxiety, sleep deprivation, and hormonal changes—can seem overwhelming.

Indeed, it is estimated that in the first week after birth about three-quarters of new mothers experience mood swings or "baby blues." The blues are generally seen for the first time about three days following the birth and can last for about two weeks. They are characterized by crying, irritability, anger, exhaustion, tension, restlessness, anxiety, and possibly insomnia.

Postpartum depression can also be triggered by other emotional and financial preoccupations. It is easy to underestimate the strain a newborn can put on your life. Again, it is good to talk to people close to you and express your worries and concerns. If you have prolonged feelings of anxiety, fretfulness, despondency, or lack of interest in your baby, contact your physician.

LOOK AFTER YOURSELF

The most important thing you can do to deal with or fend off the baby blues and postpartum depression—and to reduce the likelihood of it happening with your next baby—is to remember to take care of yourself.

Give yourself time to adjust and let all the different emotions find some form of expression. Taking good physical care of yourself is very important as well. A well-balanced diet and a mild daily exercise routine, even if it is no more than a walk around the block, will add much to your positive state of wellbeing.

COPING STRATEGIES

If you are following a self-help plan and your symptoms show no signs of improvement after two to three weeks, it is time to seek professional advice. However, before reaching that stage, you may find it increasingly hard to get through each day. If this happens, try some or all of the following strategies.

□ Talk about your feelings with your partner, family, or friends.

□ Accept or ask for help from others.

□ Rest or nap when the baby sleeps.

□ Take a break and go out for dinner or a film with your partner ... or enjoy a take-out meal at home. Meet a friend for lunch.

□ Lower your expectations of yourself right now.

□ Join a new mothers' group.

□ Exercise (with your doctor's permission).

□ Make time for yourself when your baby is asleep—read, take an aromatherapy bath, watch a video, or pamper yourself in some other way.

"When I spoke to my sister on the phone, hundreds of miles away, it was she who suggested I might depressed. I think it takes someone who knows you well to see it."

JO, MOTHER OF OLIVIA, WILLIAM, AND PHOEBE

the road to recovery

If you experience pain of any kind after the birth, don't be afraid to ask for help. Medication is usually available, but simple comfort measures can be very effective at relieving pain without leaving you feeling groggy.

SORE MUSCLES

Labor is frequently a marathon—and even a relatively short labor can lead to muscle strain and stiffness. Your hips may be sore as well, especially if you had your legs straddled for hours, or your legs were pulled into odd positions by the labor support team. If you had an epidural, your back may also be sore.

To ease these types of pain, try taking regular warm showers or indulging in soothing soaks—or resort to massage and other techniques for comfort (see pages 96–119). Gentle stretching and moving around after the birth can also bring relief. Ask your physician to advise on appropriate medication.

A TENDER PERINEUM

You are likely to be feeling tender in the perineum, the area from the vagina to the rectum, which expands to allow the birth of the baby and then slowly returns to its usual shape. If the tissues are swollen, ice packs right after birth can be beneficial. You are more likely

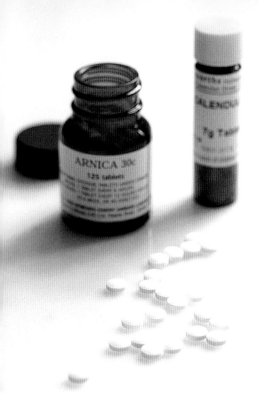

"If your breasts are hot and sore as the result of engorgement, spraying them with warm water from a shower attachment is wonderfully soothing."

KARENA, MOTHER OF SHANNON, SCARLET, AND TILLY

to have pain here if you had stitches after the birth. If a ventouse (vacuum extractor) or forceps were used during the birth, your tissues may have sustained more damage down below.

To soothe pain, bathe the perineum alternately in hot and cold water. A bath with a handful of Dead Sea salts is restorative. A warm shallow bath containing 6 drops of lavender essential oil is one of the best ways to help heal the area after stitches and to ward off infection.

Don't touch your stitches. They will usually dissolve on their own and will not need to be removed by a medical practitioner. Occasionally, a small stitch will not dissolve, but this is nothing to be alarmed about. Any swelling in the area should subside in about two weeks.

To help heal internal and external bruising, try the homeopathic remedy Arnica 30C, and to deal with soreness, particularly from an episiotomy or tear, take Calendula 30C. Sitting on an inflatable rubber ring can be a good way to get through this period of discomfort. Depending on the extent of your pain, the choice of

medication ranges from over-the-counter products to those prescribed by your doctor—but only resort to medication if you really need it. A number of painkillers may cause constipation.

BREAST PAIN

As your milk comes in, your breasts will feel full, warm, and tingly. Some women have painful engorgement, for which breastfeeding is often the best cure. You can try alternating hot and cold packs on your breasts to ease discomfort. Other remedies include applying ice-cold cabbage leaves to the breasts or soaking them in a very warm bath or shower. Avoid using a breast pump early on unless your baby won't feed. If you allow feeding on demand, your body will quickly regulate the amount of milk you produce. If pain persists, find a breastfeeding counselor, who may have other remedies of her own.

For new mothers who do not plan to breastfeed, a tight bra and no breast stimulation will provide the fastest relief during this period.

"Lavender essential oil in the bath water was a wonderful discovery— really, deeply relaxing. I sprinkled it around my bedroom, too."

SHEENA, MOTHER OF RUBY

natural remedies

There is no good reason to stop pampering yourself now that the baby has arrived. There are many natural and herbal remedies to heal, soothe, and promote wellbeing for both of you.

ACUPRESSURE

Acupressure—which was originally used as an effective treatment for various illnesses and to combat pain—is straightforward, safe, and helps to stimulate wellbeing. It has its roots in ancient Tibet, where farmers and homemakers learned to identify and focus on the channels—or meridians—that relate to physiological and energetic structures of the mind and body.

To give yourself acupressure, use your index finger or your thumb—or both together—to press down firmly on the point as you slowly count to 100. Release for a count of ten and then repeat five times.

□ To treate poor vitality and other stress-related conditions, press on the acupressure points on either side of the chest, above the breastbone.

□ To treat backache and constipation, press on the acupressure point in the middle of each instep.

□ To treat overwhelming fatigue, anxiety, headaches, and upper neck pain, press on the acupressure point in the middle of your forehead, just below your hairline.

CRANIAL OSTEOPATHY

Cranial osteopathy is said to release strain patterns caused by childbirth (birth trauma) that affect moods. All my babies had cranial osteopathy (as did I); on the whole, they are calm, gentle, thoughtful children, and I am sure that they will be the same as adults.

HERBAL REMEDIES

Arnica helps reduce bruising, swelling, and sore muscles. Take 30C every two hours or apply the cream to the surrounding area. Never allow the cream to touch an open wound. Ice cubes wrapped in a clean towel and held against the stitches can also reduce bruising.

Calendula is antiseptic, cooling, and soothing for dry skin and diaper rash. Keep a tube of the cream in your diaper bag. If you have cracked nipples, try Hypericum and Calendula (cream or tincture) between feeds.

Chamomile aromatherapy essential oil is known for its relaxing, warming, soothing properties. Add 4 drops to a warm bath or dispersed in a carrier oil (jojoba and wheatgerm are favorites) for massage. It will relax the muscles, ease pain, and calm the spirit. It heals diaper rash and cradle cap, too.

Comfrey leaf has legendary healing powers for all the body's tissues. You can infuse the herb and apply topically for any perineal tears, stitches, or general soreness in the pelvic floor. Or try soaking in a comfrey bath several times a day for 20 minutes.

Ginger root is a warming, stimulating tonic that helps to clear shock and emotional pain after labor. It is also believed to help unite us spiritually. Use a tincture or drink fresh root ginger tea.

Ginseng is renowned as a strengthening tonic and is useful during and after a difficult or prolonged labor. Take a ginseng supplement or drink the tea, to keep your energy levels up.

Jasmine and clary-sage aromatherapy essential oils have antidepressant properties, boost relaxation and help to dissipate "baby blues." Set aside 20 minutes for yourself and soak in a warm bath containing 6 drops of either oil with the aim of achieving deep relaxation.

Lavender is one of the most healing and antiseptic of aromatherapy oils. Every new mother I know who tried it said that a lavender bath two to three times a day after the birth quickly and cleanly healed vaginal stitches. Add 6 drops to warm bath water and soak for 20 minutes. Pat the sore areas dry.

Licorice (along with apricots and prune juice) is a natural laxative and helps to reduce constipation during the crucial first week after the birth. These foods pass through the breast milk and can help your baby naturally, too.

Mugwort flower essence used during and after labor is believed to help a mother connect spiritually with a baby's incoming soul. Use 2 to 4 drops on the tongue as desired.

Red hibiscus flower essence represents universal feminine power, putting you more in control. Use 2 to 4 drops as desired.

Rescue Remedy comes from the Dr. Edward Bach school of flower essence therapy. The five flowers of this formula—clematis, star of Bethlehem, rock rose, cherry plum, and impatiens—were chosen for their effect on the spirit following a shock, trauma, or any intensely moving experience. Administering a few drops to a new mother after delivery can be a grounding and unifying ritual. Use 3 to 5 drops under the tongue once or up to every 15 minutes for an hour.

Turmeric is believed to help lift a negative mood and thoughts, and to help lift depression. The acrid smell clears confusion.

Walnut flower essence helps you to release the child and the pregnancy on an emotional level, and to make a transition to the next level of your mother–child relationship. Use 2 to 4 drops as needed.

Yarrow helps to control excessive blood flow, making it ideal to have available to deal with postpartum bleeding, which can go on for weeks. Use a tincture from the herb and use 10 drops of this formula, once the placenta has been delivered, every 15 minutes until bleeding is under control.

Men often find it hard to adjust to fatherhood. Although the man has not had the physical strain of pregnancy and birth, he may experience his own form of exhaustion from changes in household schedules, interrupted sleep, increased financial responsibilities, and concern about his partner's needs. Both mothers and fathers sometimes feel disappointed if they cannot enjoy this time fully.

TEN WAYS TO... *enjoy fatherhood*

1 Remember that babies aren't breakable. Don't be nervous about holding yours. Ask someone with some experience—for example, a doctor, nurse, doula, relative, or friend—to show you a few comfortable holds for little ones.

2 New mothers have emotional ups and downs that are unpredictable. Be supportive and offer your partner an ear when possible. Learn how to recognize the warning signs of postpartum depression and seek help if you see them in your partner and the situation appears to be heading out of control.

3 New fathers, like new mothers, can experience postpartum depression. Much in your life has changed. It is important to realize this and seek help if you feel you need it, too.

4 If your partner is breastfeeding, give her as much support as you can. Tell her that you are proud of her and protect her from well-meaning but negative comments about breastfeeding from relatives and friends. Attending a breastfeeding class during the antenatal period can be invaluable. Consult your hospital about where to obtain local advice.

5 When it comes to babycare, the only thing that a new father cannot do is to breastfeed. You can change diapers, soothe a crying baby, carry the baby, play with the baby—indeed, you can deal with anything that the baby needs done. And before long you will probably be able to participate in bottle-feeding, which will give you the chance to build a closer bond with your baby.

6 If you need any expert advice or practical assistance, don't be reluctant to ask for it. Know who to contact in your area for help and support—whether it be a doctor or midwife, a postpartum nurse, a lactation consultant, or a local babysitter.

7 If you are feeling pushed to one side in a home where the needs of the new baby are given top priority, talk to your partner about it. The chances are that you are not being excluded on purpose.

8 Help as much as you can with looking after other children or running the household. Remind your partner to forget about household chores and to focus on her recovery and on the new baby.

9 Your partner is going to need extra sleep and care while she recovers from the birth and establishes a feeding routine. Get up with the baby when you can. Bring the baby to her in the middle of the night if possible. If you must go back to work soon after the birth, check in with her during the day. Perhaps surprise her with fresh flowers or a healthy take-out meal.

IO Remember that introducing a new baby to the mix is always going to disrupt your rhythm of life a bit—even if it's not your first baby. Learning to live with another human being takes time. Treat yourself to a break if you need one.

six weeks: taking stock

Now that you have a baby to care for, you need to take more care of yourself than ever—so don't miss the postpartum check-up after about six weeks. Its purpose is to make sure you are healing well and are physically and psychologically healthy and happy.

YOUR BODY

At the postpartum check, you will be examined to see if your uterus has returned to its pre-pregnancy size, bleeding has stopped, and any vaginal tears or incisions from an episiotomy or a cesarean have healed. A cervical smear may be taken, and your blood may be tested to rule out anemia or thyroid problems.

Whether or not you are breastfeeding, now is a good time to discuss any problems you may be having with your breasts. A doctor will be able to determine if you have normal lumpiness or mastitis, a painful infection.

YOUR SEX LIFE AND BIRTH CONTROL

Many doctors advise new mothers to postpone having sex until after the six-week check-up. For one thing, it may take several weeks before healing is complete. If you are experiencing vaginal dryness, which is common after having a baby—especially among breastfeeding mothers—ask about helpful creams and lubricants.

Even if you have not started having periods again, you need to think seriously about birth control. Many women believe that contraception is unnecessary if they are breastfeeding, but ovulation can resume as soon as six weeks after giving birth, even if you are nursing.

You also might need to rethink your previous method of contraception. If you are breastfeeding, you should take a progesterone-only birth-control pill, for example, since estrogen, one of the hormones in the combined pill, can interfere with milk production. If you used a diaphragm (cap) before your pregnancy, it may no longer fit properly, and you will need a new one. And because sex when there is a new baby in the house is often of the now-or-never variety, or because you may be too distracted by your new duties to remember your birth control, you might want to consider an IUD, a vaginal ring, or some other long-lasting method.

EXERCISE, NUTRITION, AND WEIGHT

There is no need to worry about losing weight before you reach the six-week milestone, but women who have not lost the weight they gained in pregnancy by six months after giving birth are more likely to be overweight or obese in the future—so the six-week consultation is a good chance to discuss nutrition and exercise with your doctor. You need to devise a healthy eating plan that ensures that you and your young baby continue to receive adequate nutrition.

YOUR FEELINGS

The six-week visit provides a perfect opportunity to ask any questions that may be troubling you. If you are very sad, anxious, or irritable, and the feelings are still there several weeks after the birth, speak up. Don't dismiss them as "baby blues"—you might be suffering from postpartum depression, which requires treatment.

If you have no desire for sex and your partner is putting pressure on you, be sure to discuss the situation with your doctor. You also may want to talk about stretch marks, breast changes, scars, weight gain, and other body-image issues. If your doctor dismisses your concerns, makes you feel uncomfortable, or does not take the time to listen, ask to speak to a nurse instead.

take it easy and sleep well

The first three months after the birth are often the hardest time for new mothers. To build up the strength and stamina to get through them, and to maintain your health and happiness, seize every opportunity to relax and take as much rest as you can.

KEEP RESTING

Lack of sleep in the period immediately after the birth is what most of us expect, since we know that a certain little someone will need feeding at various times of the night. But by the time your baby is several weeks old, a lack of sleep may be taking its toll. You may find it hard to make even simple decisions and tiredness may cloud your instincts, making you over-anxious about every little cough and runny nose. This is especially distressing if you are contemplating a return to work, but it can also affect how efficiently—and safely—you perform mundane everyday tasks. For this reason, you should do what you can to get as much rest as possible.

If you have not done so earlier, by six to eight weeks after the birth, try to instigate a bedtime ritual to give yourself the best chance of getting a good night's sleep. Once the ritual has been established, stick to it every night until a pattern is formed. It will make your life a great deal easier.

YOUR BEDTIME RITUAL

Your baby has been fed, bathed, and put to bed. Now it is your turn to indulge yourself and to get in touch again with your natural rhythms.

□ Start by having a relaxing dreamy bath. Make your own soothing bath blend from a few of the following essential oils: rose, geranium, lavender, chamomile, frankincense, and mandarin. Breathe in deeply, lie back, and unwind for 20 minutes.

□ Make yourself a relaxing cup of chamomile or fennel tea (or a fruit blend, if you prefer) and sip it as you prepare yourself for bed.

□ Place a bowl of warm water in your bedroom and in the baby's room, add 4 or 5 drops of balancing geranium oil, and let it diffuse into the atmosphere to relax you even more.

□ Play a relaxation tape or your favorite restful piece of music on a personal stereo. You may want to choose a piece of music that you can play in the nursery to help your baby associate it with sleep and bedtime.

□ Arrange your pillows and cushions on your bed so that you are in the most comfortable position (one behind your back and one under a bent knee helps to support you, for example).

CO-SLEEPING

I believe that a baby sleeping and feeding side by side with its mother is one of the most natural things in the world, and maternal instincts keep your baby safe—as long as you are not under the influence of drugs or alcohol. But always trust your instincts. There have been a few cases where a mother has accidentally "rolled over" onto her baby, but incidents like this are few and far between, and parents' smoking and drinking have been heavily implicated. Indeed, research now suggests that the extra maternal contact and feeding linked with co-sleeping reduces crying and, contrary to conventional thinking, can lead to greatly increased amounts of sleep for mother and baby. Consequently, less energy is taken away from essential infant activities such as growth and building up defenses against infectious disease.

A survey of men in their twenties who co-slept with their parents between birth and the age of five found that they had significantly higher self-esteem than those who did not, and experienced less guilt and anxiety. A similar survey of women found that co-sleeping during childhood was linked with less reticence about physical contact and affection as adults. Co-sleeping appears to promote confidence and intimacy later in life. The advantages to a mother of co-sleeping are:

☐ It gives you more time with your baby, especially if you are a working mother.

☐ It allows more sleep and more nightly satisfaction.

☐ It makes you more responsive to your baby's needs.

☐ Your milk supply is boosted in response to the increased time your baby spends suckling.

> "I had my child sleeping with me for the first five years on and off. I never regretted it. As working parents, it made us feel that we had more 'time' with our girl. She just slept like a little log between us. And we loved it."
>
> **SHEENA, MOTHER OF RUBY**

The benefits to a baby of co-sleeping include:
- More opportunity for breastfeeding (in terms of total minutes and number of nightly sessions).
- Increased amount of sleep.
- Less crying time.
- A closer relationship between baby and mother.

POWER NAPPING

The idea that everyone needs eight hours of sleep is a myth. You need what you need, and this can vary between five and ten hours a night. About 18 percent of us normally sleep less than six hours. The problem is, with a young baby, you probably need more sleep than you are receiving. If you can learn the art of power napping and get it right—that is, not allow the naps to last too long—you will experience a dramatic improvement in mental and physical energy levels.

When training yourself to power nap, first set an alarm clock to go off in half an hour's time. If you can, lie in a quiet room (ideally, sleeping while your baby sleeps) or with your feet up in a chair or rocking chair. Close your eyes, fold your arms over your abdomen, and take five very slow, deep breaths in and out. Then stretch your legs away from you, holding them tensed for a count of five, relax and take five more slow, deep breaths. Now stretch your arms down along your sides, spread the fingers, and hold for a count of five. Relax and take five more deep breaths. Repeat the exercise using your arms and legs together.

By the time you have repeated the sequence three or four times, you will be mentally and physically relaxed. Listening to seamless music (the kind with no beginning or end) on a personal stereo helps, too. If you play the same piece of music regularly to your baby before sleep, you may find that he or she develops a better sleeping pattern than you might ever have imagined. Routine helps a baby to settle more swiftly. (I used to play a piece of music called *Temple of the Forest* by David Naegle.) When the alarm goes off, get up, stretch—and you should find you feel surprisingly refreshed.

gentle **singing** and **humming** will have a soothing **effect** on you and your **young baby**

DEEP BREATHING

Therapeutic deep breathing should not be reserved for the hospital delivery suite. It is the most effective way to calm down your whole body when you are feeling tense and under pressure.

Before you start a deep-breathing exercise, vaporize essential oils of geranium or lavender in your bedroom or other private space. The vapor will help calm the multitude of emotions that you are experiencing in response to new motherhood.

□ Sit comfortably in a chair, with your back supported and your feet flat on the floor. Close your eyes. Lift your hands up straight above you, as far as you can and let your palms and fingers relax.

□ Direct all your attention into the palms of your hands and your fingers. You have the ability to feel the vibrations and energy in your hands and fingers. Think of them as antennae that allow you to "feel" sounds.

□ Now imagine that your hands and fingers are starting to tune into all the sounds and vibrations around you—people talking, rush-hour traffic, the sounds of birds in the trees, your baby's gurgling or crying—anything.

□ Remain like this for as long as you are able, and use this technique—allowing the sounds and energy to pass through your hands and fingers—to help you, relax you, and make you feel more energized.

NAUSEA INDUCED BY EXHAUSTION OR STRESS

Any number of things—including hormonal changes, low blood sugar, low blood pressure, and a diet low in vitamin B_6 and iron—can cause exhaustion or stress leading to feelings of nausea.

Homeopathy, osteopathy, and acupuncture are all effective at treating stress-induced nausea. Deep breathing (see above), yoga, or tai chi are good for controlling waves of nausea.

There are several other things you can do to ease nausea caused by exhaustion and stress.

□ Try applying pressure to the shiatsu point Pericardium 6 (PC6) on the wrist. Measure three fingers' width from the crease of your wrist, and press there for 5 to 10 seconds. Repeat three times. Travel Bands (available from drugstores) work on the same principle and can also be very effective.

□ Drink ginger tea or anything with real ginger in it, such as grated fresh ginger in a glass of hot water, to calm the digestive system.

□ Sip chamomile or peppermint herbal tea, according to your preference.

□ Take slippery elm herbal tablets or powder, which can help to soothe digestion.

□ Eat more foods rich in iron such as whole grains, figs, broccoli, prunes, and almonds, or take a vitamin B_6 supplement.

□ For severe nausea, try Nux vomica 30C, Sepia 30C, or Ipecacuana 30C three times a day for five days.

touch therapies for mother and baby

Whether it involves you and your partner or you and your baby, touch is one of the tenderest forms of communication. Touch is the loving caress, the soothing stroke, that reassures another person, however big or small, that all is fine with the world.

THE POWER OF MASSAGE

Massage is an essential part of human wellbeing, and a gentle massage can not only soothe a new mother but also may help to quieten a restless baby.

My husband, Jim, and I always massaged our babies—and, even as children, they still love it, lying very still and often falling asleep before the end.

BODY MASSAGE

Give yourself a whole-body massage, starting with your torso; then moving on to your neck, arms, wrists, hands, and fingers. Use your right hand to massage the left side of your body and limbs, and vice versa. Rub around the edge of each finger and the fingertips with the opposite palm. Next move to your inner and outer thighs, mid to lower back, wherever you can reach, then your buttocks, legs, heels, ankles, feet, and toes.

Do this as vigorously as you can for ten minutes, twice daily, for ten days, when you wake up and just before you go to sleep. It will improve circulation and body tone, help to balance the three humors, aid digestion, calm stress and, in general, enhance your body's ability to work and rest.

This massage is safe for everyone—young and old—so make it a regular health habit for you, your baby, and your family.

HAIR AND SCALP MASSAGE

Sit comfortably, close your eyes, and relax the neck and shoulders. Gently rub tiny circles along the neck and up to the nape of the neck. Then, place all your fingers in your hair, slowly massage the scalp, then lift the hair upward in your fingers and hold for a count of three. If your hair is short, pick up the hair between the fingers and close the fingers together so you feel the hair being gently pulled. Repeat several times.

FOOT MASSAGE

Rub a little oil in the palms of your hands, then pick up one of your feet and rest it on your thigh, sole facing up. Now gently stroke the entire sole using flat hands, fingers kept together. Next make a fist and very gently

knead the sole of your foot from the heel to the toes. Now take each toe and gently massage each one individually and finish by sandwiching your foot between the palms of your hands and sweep from the heel to the toes. Repeat with the other foot.

BABY MASSAGE

Most parents instinctively stroke their babies shortly after birth as a way to calm them during their first cry. Baby massage is a natural progression from this early moment of contact—especially for babies who have already had a similar experience before birth through massage of the mother's abdomen in pregnancy. It represents love, warmth, and security. One way to become attuned to the idea of massaging your baby is to join a baby massage class.

New research suggests that a little massage each day benefits a baby's health and vitality as much as it does an adult's. Choose any time of the day that suits you (after a bath is good), as long as it is not immediately after a feed, when the baby may bring up milk.

Use a plain massage oil as a lubricant, so that you can carry out massage movements without causing friction or drag. Massage without oil can be irritating, especially for a sensitive newborn. Massage your baby as for an adult body massage, but do it very gently and maintain a very slow rhythmic movement.

Jim remembers how he used to lull Olivia, our elder daughter, to sleep in her basket simply by massaging her feet. And our son, William, who spent four days in a special care baby unit, needing oxygen after a lengthy birth, relaxed and recovered quickly after constant foot, scalp, and back massage. To treat your baby to a foot massage, hold the baby's feet and ankles in the palms of your hands with your thumbs resting on the soles of the feet. Using the pads of your thumbs, gently massage the whole surface of the feet.

CHOOSING THE RIGHT OIL FOR YOUR BABY

Edible oils (vegetable or plant oils) are preferable to mineral oil for the purpose of baby massage. Mineral oil, used in some commercially produced oil, is not absorbed into the outer layers of the epidermis, leaving a greasy film on the baby's skin. This pore-sealing effect can hamper the natural functions of the skin (such as excretion and heat regulation). Mineral oil is not broken down by the body or used in the human diet, so it is not known whether babies' sucking their fingers after application represents a risk.

OTHER TOUCH THERAPIES

Osteopathy uses touch and manipulation of the skeletal system to improve the body's own healing powers and promote a sense of inner calm. Studies have also demonstrated that women and babies who are treated with osteopathy or cranial osteopathy after birth may cope better with the whole birthing trauma.

Reflexology uses massage and finger pressure on the soles of the feet to stimulate specific energy points and help restore energy flow throughout the body.

Acupressure is an oriental therapy that uses the fingers to apply pressure and stimulate specific energy points throughout the body to help stimulate circulation and lymphatic drainage.

treat yourself to a **hair and scalp** massage and repeat it several times—it is **spine-tinglingly** good; start by gently **rubbing** tiny **circles** along the neck

time for togetherness

During pregnancy you may have wondered what effect childbirth would have on your sex life. The good news is that many women find that they have better, if different, sex lives after giving birth.

SETTING THE MOOD

Leaking breasts and sleep deprivation do not make any of us feel like love goddesses, but if you find that your libido has reached an all-time low, set aside some quality time for each other. Arrange an evening at your favorite restaurant or a night away together, leaving bottles with a trusted sitter—or turn the television off and make a night of it, following the advice below. It may take more effort now, but you will both enjoy it.

WHEN CAN YOU MAKE LOVE AGAIN?

It probably would not do you any harm to have sexual intercourse within a week or two of giving birth—but it would be unlikely to be very comfortable, or enjoyable for that matter. Most doctors recommend that women wait until after their six-week check-up before having sex. But many women choose to wait longer. The vital thing is not to feel pressured about sex. Plenty of new mothers find they lose interest in making love for a while. It's perfectly normal and understandable. If this happens to you, talk to your partner about it and try to get him to understand rather than feeling unloved.

BETTER POSTPARTUM SEX

Here are some tips for enhancing your new sex life.

☐ Don't rush into anything. Take your time.

☐ Talk about your fears of sexual intercourse. You may be worried about the repair of a tear or an episiotomy. You may be concerned about how your partner feels after watching you give birth.

☐ Plan for birth control. Don't be caught two months after the birth wondering if you are pregnant again because you took a chance. In the absence of worry, sex can feel spontaneous again.

☐ Spend some time alone with your partner, even if it is just to cuddle. Having a baby may leave you feeling sensually saturated, but some special snuggling time with your lover can help to revive physical desires, even before you feel like having intercourse.

☐ Get to know each other a bit more. Remember you both have to adjust your lives to being parents, even if this is not your first child.

☐ Be spontaneous. Bedtime might not always be the right time for sex. Nor will the bedroom always be the perfect place. Add some spice to your sex life and rekindle the flame any time you can.

☐ Make sure that you and your partner take enough time to get into the mood and that you are not feeling dry, which would make sex painful. If you think you need it, use an over-the-counter lubricant rather than worry needlessly.

☐ Remember that quality is more important than quantity—so make an effort when you feel like it.

☐ Shower or bathe together. Not only will it save time, you might rather enjoy it.

☐ Exercise the freedom to say "no" once in a while. Your partner might also need the same freedom. The best thing may be to compromise. Even if intercourse does not seem appealing at this time, some good old-fashioned kissing and necking may do.

This is an emotional time for you, and it's normal to feel anxious or tense. Learning how to cope with stress will enable you to feel more in control, especially at those times when it seems as though a rather small "someone else" is in control.

TEN WAYS TO... *soothe mother and child*

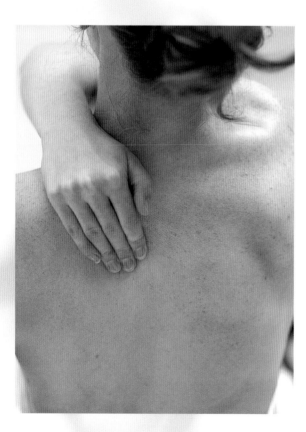

1 Give yourself a body massage (see page 32). If you do this regularly, it will improve circulation and body tone, aid balance and digestion, and generally have a calming effect.

2 Locate the acupressure point in the web of your hand between the thumb and the index finger. To relieve stress, press both sides of your hand using the thumb and middle finger of your other hand.

3 Mix 4 drops of lavender oil, 3 drops of juniper berry, and 2 drops of cypress oil in half an ounce of jojoba oil. Apply the blend to a lamp-burning ring to create an uplifting aroma in your home.

4 Combine gentle rhythmic breathing with mental imagery. Close your eyes and focus on either your contented sleeping baby or a happy, peaceful place that you love. Stay calm and peaceful, tuning into and listening to your own breathing and that of your baby.

5 According to Tibetan and Buddhist medicine, burning cinnamon sticks on a fire fosters harmony, and encourages happiness and clarity of mind.

6 Lie back, close your eyes, and picture the color red—a color associated with the entire pelvic area that relates to fear in our lives. Concentrate until you really can picture the color filling your senses. Now imagine the red filling your abdominal area and drifting down the length of your legs and out of the soles of your feet.

7 Massage your own and your baby's feet and toes (see pages 32–33). Finish each foot with a gentle sweep of the hands across the entire surface.

8 Share gentle bath infusions with your baby. Fill a small cheesecloth bag with fresh aromatic flowers such as lavender buds or rose petals, tie securely, and place it under the hot running faucet as you fill the tub.

9 A few drops of Bach Rescue Remedy in a glass of water or underneath your tongue will help you to focus and should have a calming effect.

IO Cranial osteopathy helps to rebalance the body and relieve stress and tension by the gentle manipulation of the bones of the skull, which then boosts the nervous system. Babies can be treated, too, most commonly in cases of colic or after a difficult birth.

eating and feeding

As it was when you were pregnant, your diet is particularly important now, especially if you are breastfeeding. Eating wisely will boost your health and energy, and help you regain your shape, while giving your baby essential nourishment. It will also lead you more directly along the road to inner serenity and happiness.

still eating for two?

Lack of sleep and breastfeeding are both emotionally and physically draining. You require all the energy you can get at this time—so, for your own sake, don't underestimate the importance of regular nutritious meals, especially in the first six to 12 weeks.

AN IDEAL POSTPARTUM DIET

The perfect postpartum diet is pretty similar to the healthy well-balanced diet you may have been eating while you were pregnant, with a few modifications.

If you are breastfeeding, you are still eating for two, so it is necessary to have regular meals throughout the day to maintain your energy and a plentiful supply of milk—and also to keep you in a positive and cheerful frame of mind. Even if you are not breastfeeding, lack of sleep is sure to take its toll from time to time, so you still need to eat well to recover your equilibrium.

Eating a good variety of fresh fruits and vegetables, wholegrain breads and cereals, and sources of protein is essential for any new mother's healing as well as her energy and milk supply. Eating sensibly will help you to regain your pre-pregnancy shape safely and naturally, and may prevent the onset of conditions such as adult diabetes (which is 40 percent more common if you suffered from gestational pregnancy diabetes).

Now that you are no longer pregnant, it should be fine to resume eating particular foods that you might have been warned to avoid in pregnancy. These include unpasteurized cheeses, seafood, and deep-sea fish such as tuna, halibut, and swordfish.

To boost your energy and and maintain a plentiful supply of milk, try to reduce the amount of food you consume at each meal, eating several smaller meals throughout the day rather than a few large ones.

EATING TIPS FOR NEW MOTHERS

□ Eat little and often to improve your blood sugar level and to keep it stable, making you less susceptible to "needing" sugar or mood swings.

□ Do not try to diet. Avoid high-carbohydrate or high-protein diets, choosing instead to eat a little from each food group. Eat a wide variety of foods to make sure you get everything you need to keep yourself feeling well and balanced inside and out.

□ Avoid wheat and wheat flour. Food intolerance may enhance how you are feeling at this time, so, if you are feeling low, cut out wheat because it also interferes with nutrient absorption in your intestines, which leads to bloating and discomfort.

□ Avoid stimulants such as caffeine in coffee, since this can lower the absorption of vital B vitamins.

□ Avoid alcohol. It is a simple sugar that reduces your absorption of minerals, especially magnesium, and has a dramatic effect on blood sugar level and mood swings.

LOSING WEIGHT

You will lose your weight, especially if you follow the advice given in the following pages. Eat yourself well, by eating frequently and healthily, and you will regain your shape without suffering from exhaustion in the process.

Few mothers "shrink" back to their pre-pregnancy size without paying attention to what and how much they eat—but now is not the time to get obsessed about it. As a new mother, you are likely to feel sensitive about your appearance, and you are no doubt longing to put on those slinky jeans you have been unable to squeeze into for the past six months—but be realistic.

GETTING YOUR DIGESTION BACK TO NORMAL

In the first days after you have given birth, you will be repeatedly asked by medical staff whether you have had a bowel movement. If the answer is still negative after ten days, they will become really concerned, so it is advisable in advance to increase your intake of natural laxatives such as licorice, prunes, and any other fruit,

as well as drinking plenty of water. If you have spoken to friends who have already given birth, or read any pregnancy books that tell you how it really is, you will know that your first bowel movement after birth feels exactly the same as the sensation you have when you are bearing down and pushing your baby out during the birth. Since you have only recently been through this ordeal, and everything is feeling a little tender down there, the natural reaction is: "Heck, I don't want to!" But getting your body to function properly again is a high priority, so try every method you can to make it happen as naturally as possible.

"Manon took ages to feed and preferred to fall asleep cuddling. I was advised to take her clothes off to feed. It was a real faff, but it seemed to work with her ... it certainly kept her more awake."

NATALIE, MOTHER OF LUCAS AND MANON

you are what you eat... and your baby is, too

The importance of eating well to balance your mood, to build up your strength and stamina, and to provide your baby with essential nourishment cannot be reinforced enough. Diet can also mitigate the effects of stress, allergy, and—sometimes—colic in babies.

WHY DIET MATTERS

To maintain a healthy body, we need to consume the right balance of proteins, fats, and carbohydrates, as well as adequate vitamins and minerals. Proteins form the basis of every cell in the body, and minerals are the building block of the skeletal system. Fats protect cell structures. Carbohydrates are broken down during the process of digestion to provide energy.

More interestingly, the combination of proteins and fats in our bodies provides the key to who we are as people, since these are the nutrients that the body uses to manufacture hormones—and hormones govern the way we react, our mood, our temperament, and our charisma. They are information carriers through the brain and the body, and they define individuality.

One of the essential fatty acids that affects not only our health, but also who we are is DHA. About 60 percent of the brain's dry matter is made up of fat, and most of that is DHA. The level of DHA in a mother's blood and breast milk can be raised by a diet that is high in cold-water oily fish such as salmon, cod, mackerel, and haddock.

Vital for the digestion of these essential proteins and fats is time. Taking time to enjoy your food stimulates the full quota of digestive enzymes to break it down properly. If meals are hurried, lack of efficient digestion can lead to food intolerance.

NOURISHING BODY AND SPIRIT

Experts say that breastfeeding babies take everything they need from their mothers—just as they did during the nine months in the uterus. But what about you? Vital nutrients have to be in your body in the first place for your baby to benefit from them, and to prevent you from becoming undernourished, weak, and exhausted, making you more susceptible to infection and disease—and ultimately unable to feed your baby yourself. Your

diet matters so much because it is the means by which you supply your body with the nourishment it needs to support you—your body, your mind, and your spirit.

TO BREASTFEED OR NOT TO BREASTFEED?

You will no doubt have heard the mantra that "breast is best" for babies. Breast milk contains essential nutrients that protect newborn babies from allergies and diseases until their own immune system is mature enough; and it has naturally high levels of DHA, which is vital for brain development—making "smarter babies," too. (If breastfeeding is not possible, check that the formula milk you give your baby is supplemented with DHA.)

Breast milk is also easier to digest than formula milk, and more convenient, too. No matter where you are, it is on tap, already sterilized, 24 hours a day.

But breastfeeding is not for everyone. The first two to three weeks can be particularly difficult, with sore, cracked, and bleeding nipples and endless feeding—so, if you are stressed and unhappy as a result of feeling you "ought" to breastfeed (as opposed to wanting to), then it may be time to rethink your decision. It is worth saying again that a happy mother makes a happy baby, and the relationship between you and your child does not depend on whether or not you breastfeed. You can have closeness and magical moments with a bottle-fed baby, too, and using a bottle allows your partner to help out with nighttime feeds so that you can get more rest. Right now, it is your happiness that is paramount.

NUTRITIONAL SUPPLEMENTS

You may find that breastfeeding makes it easier to lose weight after childbirth. However, the rate of weight loss after birth varies from woman to woman. Concentrate on eating a balanced diet (eating 500 calories a day more than normal to obtain adequate vitamins and

minerals for breastfeeding). Talk to your health adviser about continuing to take your prenatal vitamins while breastfeeding. Floradix herbal vitamin elixir, available online, has been consistently rated by UK and Irish midwives as the best postpartum vitamin supplement.

STRESS

Stress and the emotions linked with it—anxiety, fear, and frustration—stimulate the production of stress hormones. These disrupt digestion and may lead to irritable bowel syndrome, heartburn, acidity, colicky pain, or palpitations. Sugary foods can stimulate the stress reaction by unbalancing the levels of hormones in the body, so avoid highly refined sweet foods. Protein stabilizes blood sugar levels, so if possible eat some at every meal—eggs are an excellent source of both protein and essential fatty acids.

ALLERGIES

If you suffer from asthma, eczema, or hay fever, or if any of these conditions runs in the family, avoid cow's milk and its products while breastfeeding. If you are bottle-feeding, choose a specialized formula containing, for example, goat milk or soy milk. Cow's products may lead to irritable bowel syndrome in adults or colicky problems in babies through breast milk. Young babies do not have the enzymes needed to digest the proteins and sugars in cow's milk, which is why is should not be introduced to a baby before 12 months.

COLIC: IS IT YOU OR IS IT YOUR BABY?

Colic is a common problem in babies that is far from well understood. If you think your baby is suffering from colic, the experts to whom you turn for advice may blame, variously, your emotions, your diet (if you are breastfeeding), your stress, your baby's stress, the birth—was it too fast or too slow?

You will soon discover that anything and everything could be to blame—but you are unlikely to know the cause for sure. If you are unfortunate enough to have

a "colicky baby"—one that is apparently very "gassy" and cries like crazy for hours on end, bringing its knees up to its tummy as if in pain—rest assured that the condition usually calms down within the first 12 weeks. But you may spend those entire 12 weeks eliminating everything from your life to work out what has caused the colic—until it wears off naturally by itself.

My advice is to keep calm. Colic is common among babies. It is mysterious. The cause seems to vary from baby to baby. By all means, try out things that make you feel better about it. I found cranial osteopathy helpful if only because I felt I was taking control; my baby was clearly being helped to relax and, even if it didn't help the colic, it certainly helped me—which had to be good for my baby. There are medications you can buy for your baby, to give before each feed, which relieve gas. Alternatively, dill remedy is very effective.

Common foods linked to colic that you may want to reduce or eliminate include citrus fruits (including tomatoes) and juices; broccoli, cabbage, and other green vegetables; wheat and dairy products.

> "Cut down on 'food stressors' such as caffeine, alcohol, sugar and chocolate, and eat more 'food supporters' such as fruit, vegetables and oily fish, which have beneficial effects on mental health."

PAM PENLINGTON, NUTRITIONIST

your food and your mood

Our moods are controlled by the release of chemical messengers called neurotransmitters. We can optimize the brain processes that are used to manufacture neurotransmitters by eating the right foods—as well as by making sure we get plenty of rest and exercise.

"BLUE MOOD" FOODS

If you want to avoid a blue mood, your worst enemies are saturated fatty acids. Since they require a lot of oxygen for digestion, saturated fatty acids restrict the amount of oxygen that is transported to the brain, making you feel tired and lethargic, and even leading to depression. Many processed foods contain saturated fatty acids, including processed or fatty meats, cheese, and mayonnaise, as well as candy, pastries, and cakes.

Alcohol can also have a negative effect on mood. It seriously depletes B-complex vitamins in the body—the very vitamins we need to manufacture those chemical messengers known as "happy hormones." Restrict alcohol to small quantities—for your own sake and for your baby's sake if you are breastfeeding. Babies may become more irritable (both emotionally and physically) and less sleepy if they take in alcohol through their mother's breast milk.

Drinking any amount of alcohol and then co-sleeping with your baby is a no-no. Alcohol dampens down responses as well as moods—so, if you break this rule, you may be putting your baby at risk.

FOOD AND THE BRAIN

The brain controls all the processes in the body. To do so efficiently, it needs the following:

□ Plenty of oxygen—obtained through exercise and good nutrition.

□ Sufficient amounts of energy in the form of glucose, a carbohydrate that is best obtained from wholewheat bread, cereals, and grains; potatoes; wheat; and fresh vegetables and fruit.

□ Polyunsaturated fatty acids, which look after the protective layer around our nerve cells and transmit information as quickly as possible; these fatty acids occur naturally in cold-pressed vegetable oils, nuts and seeds, fish such as mackerel, herring, tuna, and salmon.

□ Amino acids, which are involved in the manufacture of neurotransmitters; good sources are fish, seafood, lean meat, eggs, milk and dairy products, cheese, cereals, and pulses.

□ A balanced cocktail of vitamins, minerals, and trace elements; these are present in good quantities in fresh fruit and vegetables, cereal and dairy products, lean meat, fish, nuts, seeds, and herbs.

EATING AND FEEDING

46

THE "HAPPY HORMONES"

Serotonin and noradrenalin are the most important "happy hormones"—that is, hormones that produce a feeling of happiness from within. Serotonin activates the endorphins; noradrenalin keeps the endorphins activated longer.

Serotonin promotes wellbeing and relaxation and aids deep sleep. If the brain lacks serotonin, the mood quickly sinks. A deficiency can even cause aggression. The less fat and the more carbohydrates that are available, the more serotonin is produced.

Noradrenalin, produced by the body under stress, stimulates the brain and promotes perception, energy, and motivation. Not only does noradrenalin help us concentrate in stressful situations, it can also make us feel euphoric and optimistic. It is made from the amino acid phenylalanine, found in good-quality chocolate.

Endorphins, a group of the brain's own substances that act like drugs, can reduce pain, and boost feelings of wellbeing and euphoria. A high level of endorphins makes for a balanced psyche.

Acetylcholine, a product of the B-complex vitamin choline, boosts concentration, alertness, and memory. It makes us feel mentally fit, optimistic, and relaxed.

"I NEED SOME SUGAR"

There is little doubt that eating your favorite ice cream will lift your spirits. Serotonin levels are increased by carbohydrates—and it seems that the higher the sugar levels, the quicker this mechanism works—but the effect is short-lived. Blood-sugar levels need to be kept stable by regular consumption of complex carbohydrates such as brown rice, pasta, and cereals, which provide a much slower release of energy than simple refined carbohydrates such as sugar and white bread.

KEEPING THE BLUES AT BAY

There is no doubt that what we eat plays an enormous role in how we feel, and many of us—especially new mothers—will feel a lifting of the blues when we follow a better diet. As depression affects self-perception, any alleviation of the condition can in turn boost self-esteem and even libido—but give yourself a few weeks!

While eating one particular food will not necessarily lift depression, there are links between the foods we turn to for comfort and the causes of depression.

The mechanism for boosting the neurotransmitters in the brain involves tryptophan, an amino acid that is also responsible for inducing sleep and relaxation. When we eat carbohydrates, they suppress most of the other amino acids that affect the brain and the moods; only tryptophan is believed to remain unaffected and passes straight to the brain, where it acts as a precursor to serotonin. More tryptophan increases the amount of serotonin in the brain. You can raise your tryptophan intake by eating turkey, salmon, and milk products.

"FEEL-BRIGHT" NUTRIENTS

If you want to do what you can to maintain happiness and fend off depression, increase your consumption of the following vitamins and minerals.

□ The B group of vitamins. These are especially effective at lifting mood, especially vitamin B_6, which is involved in the synthesis of serotonin, and B_{12} and B_9 (folic acid), which are needed for the synthesis of dopamine. Vitamin B_3 levels have been found to be low in people suffering from depression.

□ Zinc and magnesium. These minerals are important in the fight against depression. Magnesium is involved in the production of dopamine, and low levels of zinc are linked with depression. It is believed that postpartum depression is linked to low zinc levels, since much of the mother's zinc passes through the placenta to the baby in the days immediately before the birth. Zinc is also known as the growth mineral, and low levels of zinc in mothers of newborns are further highlighted by the concentration of zinc in colostrum, the yellowish fluid that precedes milk every time a baby is breastfed.

□ Selenium. This mineral has also been found to be lacking in people with depression.

MAKING NEUROTRANSMITTERS MORE EFFECTIVE

Among the many ingredients in our food is a handful of substances that reinforce and increase the positive effects of neurotransmitters.

□ Many spices are a tonic for body and soul, so add them as often as can to your food. Saffron boosts wellbeing. Nutmeg and cinnamon lift the mood. Vanilla and capsaicin, which gives paprika its heat, release endorphins.

□ Sinigrin, found in mustard and vegetables such as brussels sprouts and broccoli, stimulates alertness and boosts happiness and wellbeing.

□ Analeptic amines, found in oats, help to release dopamine, a precursor of serotonin.

the experience of breastfeeding

There are entire books written on the subject of breastfeeding—and, if it does not seem to be going well, it can become a very emotionally charged issue. In these few pages I have tried to focus on the essentials and what really helps.

PROS AND CONS

I was fortunate enough to breastfeed all three of my babies. For me, nothing can compare with the peace and contentment of the experience. Breastfeeding is a bonding process between mother and child, creating an irreplaceable link. I will never forgot those precious moments spent snuggling close for half an hour or so at a time, gazing endlessly at every delicate part of my baby's face, hands, feet, cheeks, elbow dimples.

But before I make breastfeeding seem like the easiest thing in the world—which, for many women, it is not—let me say that my experience was not always perfect. If you encounter difficulties, try to persevere and seek the advice of a professional breastfeeding counselor, because there is a good chance that you will succeed.

I am a fair-skinned redhead (apparently, the paler your skin, the more sensitive your nipples) and with my first child, Olivia, I was in agony with sore, cracked, and bleeding nipples. Forget about which breast was most full and ready for a feed—I would simply have to grit my teeth and put up with it each time she latched on (incorrectly, I would later learn). When I had suffered in this way for about eight days, an Irish midwife with a passion for natural remedies recommended Hyper Cal tincture. It was miraculous. Within three days my nipples were totally healed, and I could breastfeed with ease and, more importantly, with comfort. Then, and only then, did I start to love it.

My second baby, William, stayed in hospital to receive oxygen as a precaution after a lengthy birth. I couldn't feed him for the first three days, so I expressed milk to make sure my breasts had had enough stimulation to feed him once I was able. As a result, I had no soreness.

With my third baby, I achieved a great latch from the start. All my creams and potions were at hand—and she was heaven to feed from beginning to end.

PERFECT POSITIONING

Positioning your baby correctly from the very first day really is the key to successful breastfeeding.

□ Support your back at all times. Sit comfortably and lie the baby on a pillow on your lap so that her mouth is in line with the areola (the dark circle around the nipple) of the breast you have chosen to feed from first.

□ Place your baby on the pillow so that her whole body faces your abdomen and cradle her head in the crook of your arm. A swaddled baby feels more secure and may be easier to move from one breast to the other.

□ With the baby's mouth in line with the areola, gently squeeze the areola so that its shape matches the width of the baby's mouth. Then place it all in the baby's mouth. If the baby takes in only the nipple, the nipple will be very sore within 24 hours. Tickle your baby's top lip with a nipple to encourage her to open her mouth.

□ To make sure the entire areola enters the baby's mouth, it may help to spread the index finger and thumb of your spare hand and lightly place them under the breast, allowing you to support the breast and direct it more accurately.

□ Once your baby has learned to latch on effectively, try feeding while lying on your side in bed or with the baby held under one arm like a football.

□ When you have gotten used to breastfeeding, you will probably find that you do not need to use the pillow any longer. Instead, you can simply cradle your baby at the correct height.

feeding a newborn baby

Breastfeeding mothers are generally advised to allow newborns to feed "on demand." This means feeding whenever your baby appears hungry, rather than setting a strict schedule. Feeding on demand stimulates your breasts to produce more milk and ensures that the baby is well nourished.

GETTING STARTED

In the first few days or weeks, on-demand feeds occur every one to three hours (about ten to 12 sessions in a 24-hour period). In the first few days after birth, you may have to wake a sleepy baby to feed (especially if the baby is jaundiced, for example). These early feeds are often short; sometimes a newborn suckles for only a few minutes at each breast. Breastfeeding mothers should consume plenty of liquids. A useful rule is to have something to drink every time you feed your baby.

Over time, feeding sessions will lengthen. When a feed from one breast lasts for at least 15 minutes, your baby will be nourished by "hindmilk"—which contains more fat and calories than the "foremilk" that the breast produces first. You will soon begin to recognize when your baby is satisfied. You can then establish a pattern of feeding that suits you and your baby.

The mother's milk supply increases to meet a baby's needs. By day six, a newborn who is getting enough milk has six or more wet diapers and three or more mushy, yellowish bowel movements in a 24-hour period. Some babies have a bowel movement after each feed. You will learn what is a normal pattern for your baby.

By the time your baby is three months old, feeds will become quicker and less frequent. At this age the baby is able to drink more milk in one go, and your body will

adjust to the new pattern. However, a baby's feeding patterns frequently fluctuate in the first six months. Needs typically increase during growth spurts, which usually occur around the following ages: ten days to two weeks; five to six weeks; two-and-a-half to three months; and four-and-a-half to six months.

SUPPLEMENTING BREAST MILK

There should be no need to supplement a breastfed baby's diet with formula milk or food before the age of four months, even during a growth spurt. If you do give a supplement, it may reduce your milk production. A better option is to breastfeed more frequently during a growth spurt to boost your milk supply. But this is a generalization. You may find that a baby who was big and heavy at birth (as more and more babies are these days) is quite simply "hungry" at three months and needs to be introduced to baby rice, although many pediatricians prefer to delay introducing "solids" until a baby is at least four months old.

The French have customarily added baby rice to their babies' bottles to make them more contented, "full" babies. And I know that my babies all benefited from the occasional teaspoon of cool boiled water (the fontanelle—the soft area on the crown of the head where the skull has not yet fused—would dip noticeably,

breast milk alone provides all the **vitamins,**

minerals, and **antibodies** that a baby needs

which indicates that the baby may be dehydrated). I sometimes gave them a tiny quantity of chamomile tea, too, which I believe helped to soothe a colicky tummy and an overtired body—and they have all continued to love it till this day.

Research shows that, for a baby's first four to six months, breast milk alone will provide all the necessary vitamins, minerals, and antibodies. But, as a precaution against rickets, it is recommended that a supplement of at least 200 IU of vitamin D be given daily to all infants, including those who are exclusively breastfed.

You can, if you wish, continue breastfeeding until your baby is at least a year old while supplementing the baby's diet gradually with iron-fortified foods. From the age of one, a baby may breastfeed only twice daily, but if a mother decides to breastfeed beyond the first year, her baby will continue to benefit nutritionally. Ask your health professional about when to start weaning.

"One of the unsung joys of breastfeeding is that it means you can forget about bottles: no cleaning, sterilizing, endless mixing of formula, heating and cooling—to say nothing of the money you save."

HENRIETTA, MOTHER OF SOPHIE AND JAMIE

"My sister called from abroad when my first child was only three days old and my breasts were painfully engorged. The baby needed feeding but my nipples were so cracked and sore that I didn't want her near me. So I burst into tears and howled down the phone... Then I had a hot bath and massaged each breast—and quickly it all calmed down."

KATHERINE, MOTHER OF JACK AND LUCY

taking care of your breasts

It's amazing how those items of allure have now become the means of sustaining life. Just remind yourself that they are only on loan to your child—and you want them back in relatively good shape.

WASHING ROUTINE

Wash your breasts and nipples with a clean sponge or cloth and warm water only—do not use soap, which is drying. After a bath or shower, air-dry your nipples by walking around topless rather than rubbing them with a towel. If possible, do the same after breastfeeding. While you are relaxing in a bath or under a shower, take the opportunity to give your breasts a gentle massage, starting near the armpits and moving toward the nipples. Regular breast massage will help to prevent problems such as clogged milk ducts and mastitis.

BE COMFORTABLE

Wear a well-fitting, supportive nursing bra day and night. If your bra has a plastic insert or liner, remove it at night to allow air to circulate around the nipples.

Positioning your baby correctly on the breast will help to avoid soreness (see page 51). Your baby should be latched onto the breast in such a way that he or she is grasping the entire areola. If your nipples do become sore or cracked, feed your baby for shorter periods but more frequently. Breast milk is a natural soother and healer, so massage a little into sore, cracked nipples and allow them to air-dry as often as possible.

DEALING WITH ENGORGEMENT

If your breasts become engorged, apply warm towels to them for 10 to 15 minutes before feeding. Or have a shower and allow warm water to flow over the breasts for 15 to 20 minutes. Letting your baby feed frequently will help to relieve engorgement. Another remedy is to apply cold packs to your breasts after nursing to ease discomfort. Unless your baby refuses to feed, avoid using a breast pump. A pump stimulates the breasts to make more milk, which may make the problem worse.

If your breasts are too full or hard for your baby to feed from, express some milk before a feed by using your flat palms to press around the areola. It helps to do this while leaning over a bath or sink. If you want to express larger amounts to freeze in bottles for later use, acquire a good hand-held electric pump. With a doctor's approval, you can take acetaminophen (not aspirin) to ease discomfort. Relief from engorgement or sore nipples often takes 48 to 72 hours.

BOOSTING MILK SUPPLY

If you let your baby feed as long and often as he or she likes, your body should quickly adjust to producing the right quantity of milk. A breastfeeding counselor may suggest remedies such as fennel, fenugreek, and milk thistle supplements—all of which boost milk supply.

BOTTLE-FEEDING MOTHERS

If you are bottle-feeding your baby, wash your breasts daily with soap and warm water. Wear a well-fitting, supportive bra day and night for at least two weeks after the birth or after you have ceased breastfeeding. Avoid rubbing, massaging, or putting pressure on your breasts—any stimulation will boost milk supply.

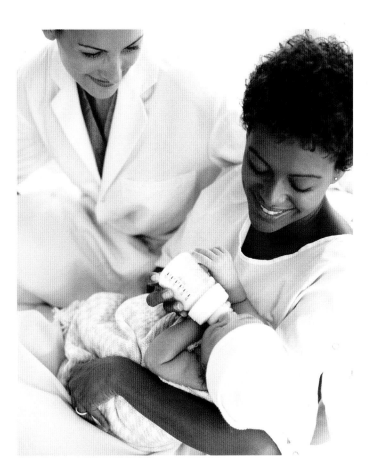

REGULAR BREAST EXAMINATION

Breast self-examination familiarizes a woman with the normal consistency of her breasts so she can identify any changes that might signal cancer. This is important because 95 percent of all breast cancers are discovered by women themselves. But bear in mind that 80 percent of the lumps that are found are not malignant.

Breast self-examinations should be done monthly, about seven to ten days after a period. In pregnancy or lactation, or after the menopause, examine your breasts on the same day each month. Your breasts will not match each other exactly. Breast tissue is more nodular during pregnancy and menstruation, and the crescent-shaped areas of firm tissue at the base of the breasts are normal. Tell your doctor immediately if you find any lumps, dimpling, swelling, or discharge, or if you note any other changes to your breasts.

quick energy sources

For a hard-pressed new mother, juices and fruit smoothies can help to curb mid-morning and mid-afternoon cravings. And it is much easier to have a drink than to try to wrestle a tiny baby with, for example, half a papaya and a spoon. There are few fruit and vegetables that cannot be blended to form a nutritious "meal in a glass," but it helps to know which, so try the recipes opposite or buy a book of juice and smoothie recipes and enjoy experimenting.

SUPER JUICING TIPS

Ask your partner, if he's willing, to make the juices for you. Perhaps he can get older siblings to help—it's a great way to make small children feel involved, and it entices them to taste, eat, and enjoy a variety of fruit.

□ Choose fruit that is not quite ripe. This yields the most juice and the best taste, and will pass more easily through the juicer than ripe fruit.

□ Use a juice extractor for citrus fruits.

□ Wash all fruit and vegetables thoroughly before juicing, but do not soak the produce because this can over-soften it and leech out some of its nutrients.

□ Freeze your fresh juice into popsicles for a refreshing one-handed juice snack in the middle of the day.

□ Turn your fresh fruit juice into a creamy smoothie by adding yogurt (or milk or soy milk to make it runnier).

ENJOYING JUICES AND SMOOTHIES AT THEIR BEST

□ Dilute fruit juices with spring water to reduce the amount of natural sugar in your diet, and alternate fruit with vegetable juice for variety.

□ To prevent juices from turning even slightly brown (by oxidization, which damages their nutritional content), drink them immediately after juicing, or pour them into a pitcher containing a squeeze of lemon juice or a teaspoon of vitamin C powder.

□ Keep unconsumed drinks covered and cool—in a sealed container in the fridge or in a thermos flask.

The quantities given in these recipes are enough to fill a pitcher or four glasses.

MEALS IN A GLASS

The recipes on this page represent just a few of the many fruit and vegetable blends that make healthy, nutritious drinks. Juices are clear and made directly from fruit that has been pushed through an extractor, while smoothies are creamier, made in a blender from the pulp of fruit, and may be mixed with yogurt.

Mango berry

Full of antioxidant vitamins C and E, zinc, beta-carotene, folic acid, iron, calcium, and phosphorus, this deliciously sweet fruity blend will fill you with energy, have a fabulous effect on your skin, and boost your immune system (especially important while you breastfeed).

  2 mangoes, peeled, stoned, and cut into chunks
  15 strawberries, hulled
  ½ pineapple, peeled, cored, and cut into chunks
  10 tablespoons natural yogurt
  10 tablespoons pineapple juice

The ginger

A great immune-system booster, this refreshing drink is packed with vitamin C, beta-carotene, folic acid, magnesium, and manganese. Add more ginger for a more intense effect. Lovely served with plenty of ice.

  2 pineapples, peeled, cored, and cut into chunks
  8 oranges, peeled and cut into chunks
  2 inches fresh root ginger, peeled

Papaya power

This lively little drink will cleanse your body inside and out and bump up your energy levels, thanks to all the vitamin C.

  4 papayas, peeled, deseeded, and cut into chunks
  juice of 2 limes
  15 tablespoons of apple juice

The veggie

A simple blend of celery and carrots pushed through a juicer creates the perfect partnership to make you feel energetic and cleansed from within. It will boost your immune system and help to clear your eyes and skin. Keep a supply of raw celery and carrots in easy reach to provide a healthy reviving snack whenever you need it.

  10 celery stalks
  8 medium carrots, peeled

Apricot energizer

Rich in beta-carotene, vitamins B_3, B_5, and C, folic acid, phosphorus, magnesium, and calcium, this juice is a powerhouse of energy that promotes good digestion and stimulates the immune system. It will also relieve constipation in the mother and, through breast milk, her baby.

  20 apricots, halved and pitted
  juice of 1 lime
  20 tablespoons of prune juice

> "I ate so badly when I was breastfeeding my
> first child, and kept on such a lot of weight,
> that I swore I'd eat better second time around.
> It made an amazing difference."

KATE, MOTHER OF HENRY AND OLIVER

satisfying meals and snacks

Healthy well-balanced meals and snacks that are easy to prepare will help to boost your immune system and keep you strong—and could encourage you to eat at more regular intervals throughout the day.

LOOK, ONE-HANDED!

It is essential to eat regularly to maintain your energy levels and keep you in a positive frame of mind. You may find it easier to opt for six small satisfying meals throughout the day rather than three larger ones.

□ Choose foods that are easy to prepare in advance of the time you eat—since your baby may need to be fed at the time you had set aside for your meal.

□ Plan meals that you can eat with one hand such as hummus and pita bread, simple sandwiches, a cup of soup, a chicken leg—fast food that is fresh and healthy.

□ When cooking dishes such as ratatouille (great with a baked potato), soups, stews, fish pie, and chicken in sauce, make double the amount that you need and freeze what you don't eat for future consumption.

□ Devise meals that taste wonderful hot or cold, such as grilled vegetables with pasta or rice, so you can eat the leftovers two days in a row straight from the fridge.

□ Acknowledge the microwave as your new best friend. It is perfect for warming up food for yourself now and for your baby in a few months' time, when he or she is weaned onto solids.

A HIGH FIVE

Make food choices count with plenty of nutrient-rich fruit and vegetables. Yellow or orange and dark-green leafy vegetables are the most beneficial to health. To enhance the variety and nutritious value of your meals, make the following substitutions.

□ Eat baby spinach and watercress rather than lettuce.

□ Eat carrots rather than celery.

□ Eat cherries rather than grapes.

□ Eat sweet potatoes rather than white potatoes.

□ Eat sugar snap peas or snow peas rather than shelled processed peas.

MORNING GLORIES

Fruit cocktail is the perfect nutritional start to the day for a new mother. The greater the variety of fruit you include in it, the more delicious it will be. Don't overtax yourself by preparing it all yourself—when necessary, buy ready-prepared fruit salads (more convenient, but more expensive). Keep a bowl of fresh fruit salad in the refrigerator for snacks and little energy kicks. Among the combinations that you could include in a fruit

"I relied on home-made pizzas, topped with all the things I love—sundried tomatoes, artichokes, nice cheeses. Eat them hot or cold—and one-handed."

KARENA, MOTHER OF SHANNON, SCARLETT, AND TILLY

salad are vitamin-rich kiwi and strawberries; raspberries, blackberries, and strawberries; oranges, apples and bananas (but avoid bananas in the first couple of weeks after the birth because they may cause constipation); melon, mango, passion fruit, and oranges.

Cereal from bran to granola to Shredded Wheat is a good source of healthy fiber—and there is no reason why cereal should be confined to breakfast time. A bowl of cereal makes a filling miniature meal in the middle of the morning or afternoon. Stick to low-fat skimmed milk, which is still healthy for you both.

Wholewheat toast with a spoonful of peanut butter is a mini-meal in one. Or have a slice of smoked salmon for a delicious wholesome treat.

MIDDAY AND BEYOND

Soups Prepare plenty of soup in advance and freeze in smaller batches, or buy ready-made organic soups (but these are often high in salt, so check the label before

you buy). Then simply put the desired quantity of soup in a cup and place in a microwave to heat it up.

Chicken drumsticks Cook eight or ten drumsticks at a time and keep them in the fridge to eat over a couple of days as healthy, protein-rich mini-meals.

Tuna melt Lightly toast a piece of wholewheat bread. Arrange flakes of canned tuna on one side of the toast, top with grated Cheddar or Gruyère, and broil under a preheated medium broiler until the cheese melts.

Mediterranean mouthful On a slice of tasty bread, pile up rocket leaves, pine nuts, and Parmesan shavings. Add a dash of French dressing, and freshly ground pepper if desired.

Salads Keep a couple of bags of ready-prepared salad in your fridge as a standby. Add salad leaves to

plain sandwiches or nibble leaves from a bowl. Never underestimate the value of salad leaves—they contain plenty of natural fluid and chlorophyll, which is extremely cleansing and revitalizing to the body.

Open sandwiches Reduce the amount of bread you need, and increase the amount of filling, by making open sandwiches on just one slice of bread.

Mozzarella, tomato, and basil salad Chop up the cheese and tomato into small pieces, so you can just eat it with a fork, and add fresh basil leaves.

Pita bread and hummus You can use pita bread as a wonderful sandwich base, but toasted it's the healthiest bread for dips, and hummus is a great protein source.

Baby bruschetta Lightly grill some slices of ciabatta bread (or similar) and cut up into bite-size portions. Rub a little garlic over the surface of the bread and a drizzle of extra virgin olive oil. Top with freshly chopped sweet tomatoes and add a few basil leaves to finish.

Cheese on toasted ciabatta Slice a hunk of Italian ciabatta bread in half lengthwise. Spread a layer of pesto sauce on each of the two halves, then place a slice of goat cheese on top of each and grill until the cheese starts to melt.

EASY SUPPERS

Couscous You can buy delicious couscous in a ready-to-mix packet that takes only a few minutes to make. Add broiled mixed peppers and shallots to the couscous, and finish with grated Parmesan. Eat hot or cold.

Pasta Choose brown pasta, which contains more fiber than white and will help to maintain your energy at a good level throughout the day. Keep jars of pesto and

you may find it easier to eat **small snacks** throughout

the **day** rather than trying to have **sit-down meals**

red pesto sauce in the fridge for a fast meal, and top with baby tomatoes. Use pasta as an opportunity to add extra vegetables—steamed, roasted, or grilled—to your diet. If you choose the vegetables well, they will be good to eat the following day, too.

Lamb kebabs Kebabs are not only delicious, but also protein-rich and quick to cook. Intersperse cubes of lean lamb (or pork or beef) with chunks of zucchini, sweet pepper, mushrooms, and shallots on a skewer. Then broil in the oven or on the barbecue.

ANYTIME IDEAS

Vegetable paella

Although it is a slight hassle to cook, paella is a dish that you can make in large amounts to keep you going for several days. The quantities given here are enough for three portions—two for dinner, one for lunch.

3 tablespoons olive oil

2 shallots

1 cup (250 g) brown rice

pinch of saffron

1½ cups (300 ml) vegetable broth

4 tomatoes, peeled and sliced

3 red and green peppers, sliced

1 garlic clove

1 tablespoon chopped fresh thyme

salt and pepper to taste

Warm the oil in a large pan, add the shallots, and gently brown. Next stir in rice, saffron, and broth, and bring to a boil. Then stir in everything else, cover, and bake in a preheated oven at 350°F (180°C) for half an hour.

Goat cheese salad

half a bag of fresh salad leaves

salad dressing

10–12 sweet cherry tomatoes

4 oz (100 g) goat cheese

This is a quick, impressive salad that is easy to make. Use a bag of ready-washed baby salad or Italian leaves (and wash them again, I would advise). Arrange the leaves decoratively on a plate, drizzle with your favorite salad dressing, such as olive oil and balsamic vinegar, and top with sliced baby tomatoes. Place a slice of goat cheese under a hot grill for a minute, or just long enough to melt it, yet keep it solid. Then simply place the melted cheese on top of the salad.

The big veggie feast

1 carrot

1 zucchini

8 baby corn cobs

8 sugar snap peas

8 baby asparagus heads

half a head of broccoli

half a head of cauliflower

Guaranteed to relieve constipation in no time, this delicious medley of vitamin-rich vegetables—lightly steamed and topped with a bit of butter—is a healthy, cleansing meal in itself. Alternatively, for an extra protein boost, you can combine it with grilled fish or a piece of grilled chicken.

SNACKS

Your need for instant energy right now is immense, but refined-carbohydrate fixes in the form of chocolates, cakes, and cookies are not the answer.

Make sure that you have plenty of healthy nibbles on hand that will prevent you from snacking on sugar. These could include nuts (brazil, almond, hazlenut, pecan, and walnuts), seeds (pumpkin, sunflower), fresh fruit, rice cakes, and crudités.

Keep your refrigerator well stocked with crudités such as sliced carrots, celery, and cucumber and eat them with dips for a satisfying mini-meal. Choose from guacamole, taramasalata, red-pepper hummus, and sour cream and chives.

Whether or not you have recently had a baby, one secret of good nutrition is to learn how to savor your food. Choose your ingredients wisely and enjoy every mouthful. Above all, don't rush your meals.

TEN WAYS TO... *eat better*

1 Eat slowly and chew food well. A meal or snack should take 20 to 30 minutes to eat. Wait 15 minutes before taking a second helping.

2 When choosing carbohydrates, look for high fiber. Fiber—especially insoluble fiber—aids digestion and can lower LDL or "bad" cholesterol by adding more HDL or "good," artery-cleaning cholesterol. Go for bulgar rice, bran cereal, wheatgerm, oats, and kidney beans.

3 Experiment with various cooking methods—try roasting or broiling vegetables (especially zucchini, peppers, carrots, parsnips, mushrooms), or steam them for a few minutes to preserve the most nutrients.

4 Always eat at the table. Avoid eating in front of the television or while reading. If you focus on your food, you will desire less quantity and more quality.

5 Eat a variety of foods and discover how to use spices creatively; flavor is not synonymous with fat.

6 Eat vegetables raw, if you can. And try to buy organic. You can get organic "anything" now if you hunt hard enough—nuts, rice, pasta, cookies—and it's the best option for babies and children, too.

7 Don't eat finger foods by the handful. Eat them piece by piece to enjoy the holistic experience of eating.

8 Limit treats and refined foods; minimize your salt intake; reduce or avoid alcohol and caffeine; and avoid fizzy drinks and chemical foods.

9 Schedule all your meals and snacks, and eat them as intended. It is important not to skip meals or to "save up" for one big meal.

10 Prepare your lunch in the morning after breakfast when you are not hungry and tempted by food. Prepare fruits and vegetable snacks in advance of eating them—in this way, you will be less likely to be tempted by sugary snacks.

the fittest you can be

Even the shortest bursts of daily exercise can do wonders for your mind and spirit as well as your body. Health and vitality are especially important to you right now because there is a small person who is dependent on you. So be the fittest and best you can be, both for yourself and for those who need you most—and enjoy the experience.

why exercise matters

Are you content to snuggle down indoors and immerse yourself in the glory of motherhood? Or do you long to get up and get out? There is no right or wrong approach for a new mother to take—but, if you are feeling low or cooped up, regular exercise can work wonders, as well as greatly improving your chances of losing weight and regaining your pre-pregnancy shape.

ENERGY

If you spend all day lounging around the house, you probably won't feel like bounding out of bed the next day . . . and so the endless round of life with a newborn continues. Conversely, if you take regular exercise, even if it's no more than a daily walk, you will have more energy, not less—and tiredness will be a good feeling rather than a sluggish exhaustion that knows no end.

PHYSICAL HEALTH

Exercise provides untold benefits for your heart, muscles, lungs, circulatory system and digestive system, and can help you to improve your diet by avoiding sugary carbohydrates. So start exercising and watch your blood pressure, weight, and cholesterol drop.

MENTAL HEALTH

Exercise stimulates the brain to release endorphins—the chemicals that make us feel good when we are happy and in love. So, if you are feeling down, don't sit down. Get up, get out, and get moving. Exercise—especially aerobic exercise such as walking, jogging, or running—has been shown to be effective in reducing depression and anxiety. It also increases mental concentration and clarity, and makes you more alert and energetic. This is vital for a new mother, who needs to keep a watchful eye over a small baby who will soon be on the move. If you exercise, you will feel less stressed. You will also sleep more soundly and ultimately require less sleep.

SELF-ESTEEM

Whether your self-esteem is sky high or rock bottom, you will feel better about yourself when you exercise. Increasing your physical strength will give you a greater sense of security and control. Create small goals for yourself, and as you achieve them, you will realize that you can change your life in and out of the gym. Try a new activity, sport, or regime to broaden your mind and boost your confidence.

YOUR METABOLISM AND YOUR WEIGHT

Your metabolic rate encompasses all the processes that produce energy in your body—essentially, the burning of calories—so it is intimately associated with weight and exercise. Regular exercise builds lean tissue in the form of muscle. The more muscle you have, the higher your metabolic rate. The higher your metabolic rate, the more calories you burn. Even though the metabolic surge may seem minimal—amounting to, say, an extra 100 calories burned a day—over the course of a year

exercise increases **mental concentration** and **clarity** and makes your more alert and **energetic**

that adds up to 10 lb (4.5 kg) worth of fat lost. One of the most wonderful effects of exercise is to raise your metabolic rate during periods when you are not exercising, such as while you are asleep.

A HEALTHY THYROID

Thyroid dysfunction can happen at any age, although it is commonly associated with people aged 40 and over; it affects one in six women before the age of 60. It is particularly common in mothers after a second or third baby, setting in at around 4 months after the birth. For some women it may be temporary, but for others it is a permanent condition requiring lifelong medication.

The thyroid, a butterfly-shaped gland at the front of the neck, produces hormones vital for the regulation of metabolism, helping every cell in every tissue and

organ in the body to work perfectly. Hypothyroidism occurs when the thyroid is underactive and unable to produce enough of these hormones. It is often caused by Hashimoto's thyroiditis, an "autoimmune" condition in which the body's own antibodies gradually reduce the hormone-producing cells in the thyroid gland. The result is a decrease in metabolic rate and a gradual slowing down of both physical and mental functions. The symptoms include general tiredness, weight gain, poor memory, muscle weakness, poor concentration, unexplained crying, depression, and extreme sensitivity to cold. Since many of these factors are common in new mothers, the condition can go undiagnosed.

Hyperthyroidism, by contrast, occurs when the thyroid is overactive, producing more hormone than is needed. It is sometimes described as "driving with the choke out"—you get extra power, but pretty soon you run out of fuel. And, since the metabolic rate goes into hyperdrive, people with the condition often lose weight and suffer from an irregular heartbeat and palpitations.

BODY IMAGE AND AWARENESS

Self-image is shaped by influences and experiences that can be complex and profound. If you exercise and eat well, you will become more aware of your body—how it works, moves, and feels.

Take a long look at yourself in a full-length mirror. Instead of having self-deprecating thoughts about your floppy tummy, cellulite, and excess weight, flex your muscles. Think of the power of the human body—your body. Marvel at its strength and power, at the length of your legs and the strength in your arms. Concentrate on the miracle of what your body has achieved through childbirth, and congratulate yourself over and over again. Now visualize how you will look and feel in a few months' time, once you have mastered the art of breastfeeding and your milk supply has settled into a pattern, along with your baby's routine. The following tips may help to boost your self-image and self-esteem at times of low motivation.

Seek balance Don't become obsessed about how you look and what you are eating. Try to enjoy a variety of activities, which might include reading or painting. Discuss your worries with a close friend.

"I'm only 35, but since having my second baby I am two sizes bigger than I used to be, and I can't bear not being able to wear lovely fashionable clothes that show off my figure the way I used to. I seem to look mumsy and frumpy all the time."

SANDY, MOTHER OF LARA AND BELLA

Love yourself Accept yourself for who you are today, here and now. Goal-setting should not be a rejection of your body, but a plan to make it healthier.

Focus on the means, not the ends It is the journey that matters, in the end. Think about the good food you have eaten, not the naughty things, or reflect on the walk you enjoyed in the fresh air with your baby, rather than on the pounds you want to shift. Enjoy the journey—you will get there more steadily.

Focus on the positive Think of features of yourself that you like or that are often admired, such as bright eyes, fabulous hair, or a great smile. Then aim to add one more and give attention to that—neater nails or perfectly pedicured feet, for example.

Remember who you are You are a mother now, but you are still you. So focus on your accomplishments and attributes in every area of your life, from being a great friend to being a good cook or a creative person.

exercise dos and don'ts

If you had a normal vaginal delivery and are feeling strong and well, you can begin gentle exercise before the conventional landmark of the postpartum examination at around six weeks. The only activities that should be restricted are any that involve extreme stretching or balancing acts, and unusual positions, including some yoga poses. Slow does not always mean safe, so take plenty of care.

AFTER A CESAREAN

If you had a cesarean, you may be offered specialized postpartum physiotherapy or an exercise sheet to follow. You will be advised to start with breathing exercises and ankle circling to boost blood circulation. Soon you will be able to do pelvic tilts lying on your back, progressing slowly to more strenuous exercise.

WHAT YOU CAN DO

Whatever type of delivery you had, aim to re-establish gradually a semi-normal "old" routine. It is important for your body and your self-esteem slowly to resume the activities you were used to doing before pregnancy, provided that they are safe and you experience no discomfort. Listen to your body and get approval from your doctor before starting any new fitness regime.

Introduce exercise into your daily schedule as early as possible. It will give you something to look forward to and help to reduce the monotony of a newborn's schedule of sleep, feed, play, sleep, feed, play, sleep.

Even if, at first, you can walk for only a short period while pushing the buggy, it is valuable to develop what is known as the Stroller Stride. Begin slowly. Decide on a destination and a safe public route, and set yourself a pace and a goal, becoming slightly more ambitious each week. You will get better and fitter progressively. Ask your partner or a friend to help you carve out

you will need your **partner** or a trusted **relative** or friend to look after the **baby** while you **exercise**

some time—all it needs is 20 minutes a day. Apart from anything else, short periods of exercise will give you the opportunity to think and plan, and will help you to maintain your equilibrium at this challenging time.

STEPPING OFF

Walking can take you from those first few weeks after delivery into a full-fledged fitness plan. To get the most from your walk, invest in a comfortable pair of walking shoes and carry a water bottle to keep hydrated.

Concentrate on your posture while you walk. Walk tall with your stomach tight (as much as possible). Lift your chest, relax your shoulders, and keep your head up. Step with your heel first, then roll to the ball of your foot and push off your toes for more power. Strive to walk for 20 minutes a day (20 minutes is the ideal

length of time to exercise before your body starts to burn body fat), gradually increasing your pace and distance as the weeks progress.

SWIMMING

Swimming is an all-round aerobic exercise that you can do at your own pace, and which exerts no load-bearing strain on your body. (To avoid infection, wait until all stitches have healed.) Even if you can't swim, you can exercise in the pool by holding onto the side with your back to the wall and cycling in the water, or by facing the side of the pool and swaying from side to side.

YOGA AND OTHER EXERCISES

Yoga-based exercises improve suppleness and flexibility, and encourage deep-breathing to boost relaxation. As

"The pressure was on to go back to work with a tiny waist, as trim as possible. So, on the dot of six weeks, I was back in the gym three times a week pounding away, and within four weeks my waist was back, and everything was looking more 'me' again. I was so happy."

LUCY, MOTHER OF HARRY

with all exercise at this time, it is wise to proceed with caution. Find a qualified postpartum yoga teacher and avoid overstretching loose muscles.

Postpone strenuous activities such as brisk walking aerobics, running, and jumping until six weeks after delivery, and also forgo intense abdominal exercises for six weeks to give the uterus and any incisions a good chance to heal, and to avoid overstraining muscles and ligaments. However, as soon as you feel comfortable, resume the Kegel (pelvic-floor) exercises that you were advised to do in pregnancy (see page 76).

WHAT YOU SHOULDN'T DO

Don't overdo it. Your body has been through an ordeal and needs time to recover. Keep active, but be sensible, and don't overstretch yourself.

□ Running or jogging puts too much strain on the pelvic floor and around the uterus, especially after birth when there is already a lot of healing required.

□ If you had an episiotomy or experienced any vaginal tearing during the birth, avoid exercises or strenuous movements that may cause discomfort. Avoid squatting movements until the perineum is totally healed.

□ Cycling, riding, or using a stepper machine in a gym, and floor exercises such as lunges should be avoided for the first four to six weeks after giving birth.

WHO'S HOLDING THE BABY?

To begin with, you will need your partner or a trusted friend or relative to look after the baby while you exercise. Nurseries are available at some gyms for babies aged from three to four months. For a gym visit, take an exercise support bra, breast pads, incontinence pads, and toiletries. For your baby, take bottled milk (unless you are breastfeeding), diaper-changing equipment, a change of outfit, and a favorite toy.

If you are breastfeeding, be aware that the level of lactic acid in breast milk changes during exercise—and babies notice the difference in flavor. To avoid feeding problems, allow 30 minutes to an hour after exercise before you start to breastfeed. Alternatively, offer your baby some expressed breast milk from a bottle.

GET MOTIVATED

One of the best ways to get motivated in the first few weeks after the birth is to find an exercise partner, ideally another new parent. If you haven't met any new parents yet, contact an organization with a network of local groups, so you can get to know like-minded individuals. Socializing with a group of this type will help you feel more like an individual and less like "just a new mother." Arrange to meet the others on the way to the park or go shopping together.

EXERCISE DOS AND DON'TS

kegel exercises

Many of us take our pelvic-floor muscles for granted. But, if you want to remain continent well into old age, start exercises early in pregnancy and resume as soon as possible after childbirth.

STRESS INCONTINENCE AND PROLAPSE

New mothers often experience uncontrolled urinary leakage after giving birth, and several days later still have an uncontrolled leakage when laughing, coughing, or sneezing. Known as stress incontinence, this is the direct result of carrying and pushing out a baby. To avoid continuing problems, I cannot emphasize enough the importance of Kegel exercises for the pelvic floor. (They are just as important after a cesarean as they are after a vaginal delivery.)

Since the opening at the top of the vagina may not be as tight as it was before delivery, some new mothers may eventually experience a prolapse (falling) of the uterus or the bladder into the vagina. If this happens, you will feel reduced bladder control, incontinence, or stress incontinence. You will also feel a loss of tightness of the vaginal wall, with reduced pleasure during sexual intercourse, and pressure in the pelvic area, as if your bladder is pushing on the vagina. Seek medical advice.

HOW TO DO KEGEL EXERCISES

Pelvic-floor exercises will hurt at first because your entire pelvic area will be sore as a result of the birth. But the sooner you start them, and the more you do, the better your chance of regaining a "watertight"

bladder. The pelvic-floor muscles also control your "grip" during sexual intercourse—so, if you keep them fit, you may improve your sex life, too.

Imagine that you are urinating and you want to stop the flow. The muscle contraction that you would use to do that—an upward and inward pull—is the one to practice to get your bladder control back to normal. Contract the muscles, hold for a second or two, then release. Repeat. Start by doing half a dozen "pull-ups" and build up to 20 or so per session, holding in the muscles for longer each time.

Don't practice this technique while you are actually urinating, or you may encourage an infection such as cystitis. The exercises are not hard, but as in any muscle-building program, they need to be done regularly.

Barbara Olive, an holistic therapist, taught me how to pinpoint the pelvic muscles precisely. Imagine that you have a little trumpet between your legs and that you are sucking up air through the mouth of the trumpet. Suck, suck, suck the air up, then, once you have taken in as much air as you can, blow it away down your legs. Then begin again. Repeat ten times, and ideally do the exercise ten times each day. Alternatively, you can buy cones, small vaginal weights which, when placed inside the vagina, help to exercise the pelvic floor.

"After my second child, my midwife advised using cones—I simply inserted them every morning for 15 to 20 minutes while getting ready in the morning. Within six weeks I noticed a huge improvement."

DIANA, MOTHER OF JAMES AND OLIVER

fitting exercise into your daily routine

Small amounts of physical activity throughout the day can be as beneficial to your fitness and wellbeing as a longer workout.

SLOWLY BUT SURELY

If you gradually build up the amount of exercise you do each day, expect to see and feel the difference quickly. Almost instantly you should feel more energetic and be aware of an improvement in your self-esteem. Within a month, you will notice an increase in your level of fitness. You will be able to walk farther, walk upstairs with increasing ease, and have more energy for daily activities. Within six weeks, you should see the weight gained in pregnancy begin to drop away and notice a marked improvement in muscle tone.

EASY WAYS TO TAKE EXERCISE

☐ Walk to the corner store, bank, or post office with your baby in a sling rather than going there by car.
☐ Park your car at the farthest end of the lot from the stores.
☐ Walk up stairs rather than using an elevator.
☐ Take your baby for a walk in a sling or a stroller at least once a day.
☐ Travel by bus or other form of public transportation— and set your baby a good example. Many of today's babies and toddlers are driven everywhere, with the result that we are creating couch potatoes from an early age, and it is getting harder and harder for each new generation to take exercise.
☐ Pay regular visits to a local park or swimming pool with your baby. Regular physical activity is a good habit to get into, and whatever improves your mood will probably have the same effect on your child.
☐ Play games with your baby. Any stimulation will benefit the baby as much as it does you.

☐ Dance. Whether out with your partner or at home with your baby, dance yourself silly.
☐ Walk to a friend's house for a visit and to say hello, rather than going by car.
☐ Spring-clean your home—you will be improving your environment and taking exercise at the same time.
☐ Do your pelvic-floor exercises, wherever you are, as often as you can.

a healthy posture

The classic posture of the expectant mother—shoulders back, bump thrust forward—may be the only one that makes you feel comfortable. However, the "bump" is no longer inside the womb, but now being jiggled up and down on your shoulder, so it's time to adopt a healthier posture that puts less strain on your back.

A STRONG ABDOMEN

Poor posture, tension, and carrying the extra "load" of pregnancy all contribute to back strain—and after the birth you will find that rocking your baby, slouching while breastfeeding, or carrying your baby in a sling, to say nothing of a great deal of lifting and carrying, are imposing a new kind of strain on your back. So start strengthening your abdominal muscles as soon as you

can—the abdomen is your powerhouse, and the key to a strong physique. Following the advice on these pages will help you to get back into shape.

A STRAIGHT BACK

Avoid slouching. Whether walking, standing, sitting, or breastfeeding, always try to keep your back in a straight line. Don't stand with all your weight on one leg—try to

keep your weight evenly distributed. To relieve back strain, try the following gentle stretching technique, which also strengthen abdominal muscles. Kneel on all fours, with your hands and knees a short distance apart, and breathe in. As you breathe out, gently arch your back, pushing your head down so you feel a complete stretch (see opposite). Breathe in as you bring your head up. Breathe out and relax. Repeat ten times.

BACK MASSAGE

If you develop a sore back, ask your partner to give it a massage with this relaxing blend: up to 10 drops of ylang-ylang, lavender, geranium, or patchouli oil in 4 tablespoons of jojoba or sweet almond carrier oil. Alternatively, use your index and middle finger and press along your shoulders on each side, at small intervals. Repeat as often as you can. At the same time, rotate your head to relieve tension.

LIFTING TECHNIQUE

When you pick up your baby from a crib or the floor, do not bend, stoop, or overstretch yourself. Instead, sit or kneel to bring your whole body down to the baby's level. Use a changing table that is mear your elbow level (but swap to a mat on the floor by the time the baby is starting to roll). In some circumstances, it may be more comfortable to sit yourself down to the baby's level, especially in the first few weeks after a cesarean.

When lifting an object, squat down, pick it up, and hold it as close to your body as possible. When standing up, keep your back straight and use your legs muscles to do the lifting. Do not try to lift anything heavy.

CARRYING YOUR BABY

A well-designed baby sling will keep the weight of your baby evenly distributed, and is a better mode of transportation than propping the baby on one hip. In the first three months after the birth, a sling is the ideal way to carry a restless baby, indoors or outdoors, and get chores done at the same time—even tasks such as vacuuming or making yourself a sandwich. The best slings support the baby's bottom from underneath.

GETTING UP FROM THE FLOOR

From lying on the floor, roll onto your knees and use your thigh muscles rather than your stomach muscles to lift you up. This will place less stress on your abdominal area while it is recovering from the birth (especially important if you have had a cesarean).

BREASTFEEDING

Breastfeeding can put a lot of strain on your back, so it is important to establish a comfortable breastfeeding position from the very first day. An excellent tip I was given came from Claire Kedvies, one of Britain's top breastfeeding counselors, who is based at Guy's and St Thomas's Hospital in London. She advised me to place a pillow on my lap and lie the baby on top. This elevates the baby to the same level as the nipple, rather than obliging the mother repeatedly to lean over the baby, which leads to rounded shoulders and a tense back. A comfortable position will encourage you to adopt a good feeding pattern so that your nipples will be less prone to soreness. I always pass on this tip to friends with new babies.

whether **walking**, standing, sitting, or **breastfeeding**, always try to **keep your back** in a **straight line**, and keep your weight **evenly distributed**

Exercise has restorative powers. It increases your oxygen intake, which is good for you and your baby, and will leave you better able to relax than if you choose to slump on the sofa for the afternoon. Here are a few tips to get your workout working for you.

TEN WAYS TO... *exercise well*

1 Restart your exercise regime with two basic exercises: walking and pelvic-floor work.

2 You can begin some gentle walking almost immediately after the birth, but make sure it is just enough to get you breathing more heavily than normal, and stick to just 20 minutes.

3 For the first two weeks, pelvic-floor exercises should consist of a contraction lasting 10 to 15 seconds repeated five to six times twice a day (see page 76). Build up to doing them as often as you can remember.

4 Don't start dieting heavily, particularly if you are breastfeeding. You will feel tired enough from reduced sleep and the effect of feeding itself, so the last thing you need is to be taking in less food than you really need. Your baby will also suffer if you don't give yourself the necessary calories while breastfeeding.

5 Drink plenty of water. You will have lost a large quantity of water during the birth itself so it is important to keep on replenishing your reserves. During breastfeeding you will also be losing a great deal of fluid, so keep yourself well supplied. Drink a minimum of eight 8-ounce glasses (2 liters) of water each day.

6 By the third or fourth week after the birth, as long as you have had no complications, you can increase the intensity of your workout and introduce resistance exercises. You can now walk at a fast rate and work your heart up to a level of 85 percent of its maximum. Start by adopting a one-minute-high, one-minute-low format (that is, walk fast for 1 minute, then walk more slowly for 1 minute, and so on). If you feel dizzy the first few times, don't push yourself.

7 Perfect the Stroller Stride: make the most of your time pushing the stroller and stride out. As you push, try to drive the legs strongly back behind you and use your buttocks and hamstrings more effectively. Take turns with your partner pushing the stroller at a fast pace for 2½ or 3 miles (4 or 5 kilometres).

8 For a gentle aerobic workout, dance with your baby. As you get stronger, you can use lunges as an exercise to work your legs at the same time as keeping moving and rocking your baby to sleep. If you do 15 to 20 lunges on each leg for 3 or 4 sets, your baby will normally be asleep by the end.

9 Work on your core strength areas every day. The change in postural pressure that you have just been through means that your back is likely to be fairly unstable. There is still a large amount of the hormone relaxin in your system (which relaxes the muscles and joints in preparation for labor), so you need to make sure you are creating stability around the spine, or it can become hypermobile. Spend 10 minutes doing exercises to make sure you are strengthening the entire back and abdominal area as much as possible.

IO Get as much rest as you can. You will get very tired, so take power naps (see page 30) to make sure you are regaining your strength. If you really want to lose weight, being tired will not help you do it.

gentle stretches

Many new mothers store tension in the neck and shoulders, especially while seated or remaining in one position. If you work on elongating your body with gentle stretches, you will be able to break bad postural habits even at a time when most of your attention is focused on your new baby.

REGAINING YOUR STRENGTH

In pregnancy the hormones estrogen, progesterone, and relaxin increase to around 100 times their normal levels and return to their normal levels once you have had your baby. Their role is to create the conditions to help a woman to maintain her pregnancy and nourish the baby. They are responsible for making the muscles and ligaments soft and relaxed to allow the baby to grow inside the mother.

The hormonal changes that occurred in preparation for childbirth need to be taken into account when it comes to planning a post-pregnancy exercise routine. In the weeks following the birth, your body is not yet yours again. The increase in these hormones means that you are still much more supple than usual: your body becomes much looser very quickly—too quickly, if you are not careful. This mobility is noticeable during stretching exercises, such as yoga, during pregnancy, but your joints can become too unstable, and if you

fail to keep your abdominal muscles toned, the back, in particular, may be put under excessive strain. The Pilates-based strengthening exercises described on the following pages are fine to do as soon as you feel up to exercising. They place no heavy demands upon your pelvic area, but are the first step to getting your body back into shape.

HEEL LIFTS

This exercise strengthens the back muscles. The top part of the body should be totally relaxed, so don't allow any tension to creep into your back, neck, or shoulders.
1 Lie face down on the floor with a cushion under the abdomen and a smaller one between the thighs. Rest your forehead on your hands, turning your head to one side for comfort. Breathe in. As you breathe out, pull your navel toward your spine and squeeze your pelvic-floor muscles while squeezing the cushion between your thighs using the muscles at the base of the buttocks

refresh mind and body by practicing deep **breathing** whenever you can. It sends **freshly** oxygenated blood through **your** body and boosts **mental clarity**

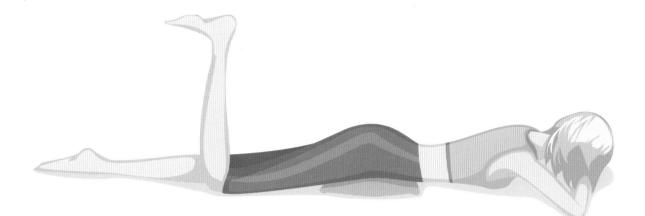

and the inner thighs. Hold this position for the rest of the exercise, keeping everything else relaxed.

2 Breathe in. As you breathe out, bend your right knee with your foot flexed and bring it as far back toward your bottom as you can. Move slowly and feel the stretch in your hamstring as you tighten your buttocks and abdomen.

3 Breathe in and lower your foot.

4 Repeat ten times on each side. If you find that you are losing the tension, reposition your abdominal and buttock muscles, but only attempt to do what feels comfortable. You will get stronger with practice.

ARM TONER

This is a simple yet effective way of toning arms. Keep your neck and shoulders relaxed. If tension creeps in, do some shoulder circles (see page 85) and start again.

1 Sit comfortably on a cushion, legs loosely crossed. With your back straight (it may help to sit against a wall to begin with), pull your navel to spine and lift and stretch your arms out to your sides at shoulder height.

2 In this position, flex your hands and fingers up as far as you can, keeping your wrists in position, so that your fingers are straight and pointing upward. You should feel a stretch all along the underside of your arms.

3 Tighten each hand into a fist and bend downward from the wrist (which still stays in the original position), almost as if they are curling back toward your body as far as they can go. You should feel a strong stretch along the backs of the hands, wrists, and forearms.

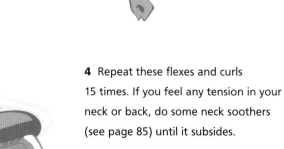

4 Repeat these flexes and curls 15 times. If you feel any tension in your neck or back, do some neck soothers (see page 85) until it subsides.

ROLL DOWNS

As well as being very relaxing, this exercise is excellent for realigning your spine and improving posture. Stop and rest if you experience any dizziness.

1 Stand 6–8 inches (15–20 cm) from a wall, with knees slightly bent and feet hip-width apart, toes facing forward. Stretch out the length of your spine, vertebra by vertebra, against the wall and keep your head held high, shoulders relaxed. Let your arms hang loosely by your sides, and pull your navel toward your spine.

2 Breathe in. As you breathe out, pull up the muscles of your pelvic floor and drop your chin to your chest, feeling the stretch all the way through your neck and upper back. Allow your arms simply to hang.

3 Deepen the curve of your shoulders and upper back as you peel your back away from the wall, head and arms hanging down, until only your bottom is touching the wall. Breathe calmly in this position for a count of ten (if possible) and relax into the stretch.

4 On the next exhalation, with your navel pulled in toward your spine and your pelvic-floor muscles pulled up, unroll yourself slowly back up into the standing position, feeling almost every vertebra touching the wall as you go. Feel your shoulders drop naturally as your back unrolls. As your head lines up with your spine, check that your neck and shoulders are relaxed and your abdomen is pressed back toward the wall.

5 Relax and breathe. Repeat twice.

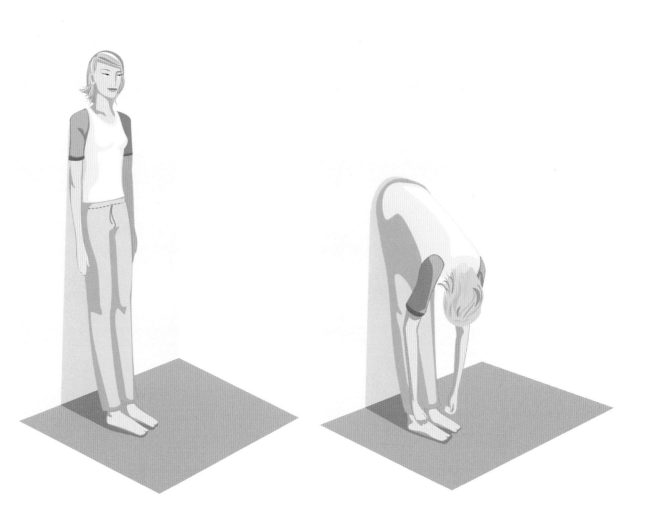

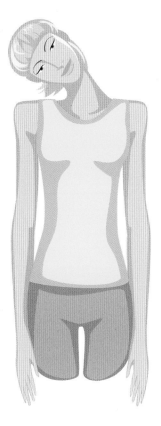

NECK SOOTHER

If breastfeeding is creating tension in your neck, this exercise should bring some relief.

1 Sit with your feet flat on the floor with a long straight back. Pull your navel toward your spine as you pull up your pelvic floor. Check there is no tension in shoulders, neck, or face. Breathe in deeply and relax.

2 Drop your chin down to your chest, without moving or tensing your shoulders. Roll your head around to the right until your ear is above your shoulder. Slowly roll it back to the center and then continue to the left.

3 Repeat three times on each side, and continue to keep everything nice and relaxed. Return to the central position and raise your head.

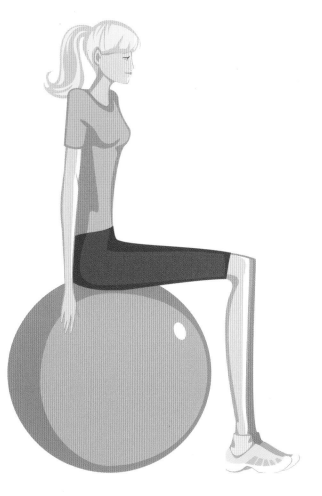

SHOULDER CIRCLES

This exercise helps release the upper body from stress, especially the back, shoulders, and neck.

1 Sit with feet flat on the floor and a long straight back. Breathe in several times and relax. Tilt your chin down slightly, keeping your neck in line with your spine.

2 Lift your shoulders as high as you can toward your ears, leaving your arms hanging loosely by your sides. Then let your shoulders drop heavily. Do this five times. Next raise just one shoulder at a time, repeating the movement five times. Repeat for both shoulders.

3 Draw your shoulders forward so that you close up the front of the chest. In a long slow movement, circle your shoulders up toward your ears and then back, as if you are squeezing your shoulder blades together. Repeat five times, then reverse the direction of your shoulder circles so that you start with the shoulder blades together and circle forward instead.

GENTLE STRETCHES

yoga for relaxation

This sequence of yoga exercises is all about seizing ten minutes a day for yourself. Try to claim the same time each day—early evening or after the early morning feed, for example—and use this period for peaceful stretching, calming, and even a bit of soul-searching. Leave your baby in its crib or on a mat under an activity arch, and have a go—but take it slowly and never overstretch yourself.

SUN SALUTATION

The "salute the sun" yoga ritual is a top-to-toe body stretch that should energize your body, making you feel more alert and in control. Many experts regard it as the perfect start to any day. It takes little time to learn, and you can do it at your own pace—for example, you could start by working regularly on the first three movements before moving on to the more demanding positions later in the sequence.

1 Stand upright with your shoulders relaxed, back straight, abdomen pulled in and feet together. Press the palms of your hands together in front of you at chest level. Hold this position and breathe in smoothly and deeply three times. On the last breath out ...
2 Stretch your arms up above your head, palms still pressed together. Hold this position and breathe in smoothly and deeply three times. On the last breath out ...

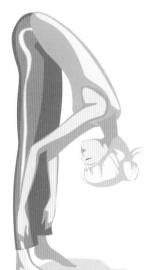

3 Bend forward from the hips and clasp your ankles. Bring your head as close to your legs as is comfortable and let it hang heavily. Breathe in three times. On the last breath out ...

4 Place one hand on the floor on each side of your feet, bending your left knee at a right angle as you stretch your right leg out behind you. Straighten your right leg by pushing the heel down toward the floor. Breathe in three times. On the last breath out ...

5 Stretch your left leg back as well, placing your feet hip-width apart, and lower your torso to the floor while raising your head and chest upward. Breathe in three times, and on the last breath out ...

6 Raise your bottom while bringing your head between your arms to create an inverted V shape with your body. Breathe in three times. On the last breath out ...

7 Raise your head and bring your right leg up, placing your foot on the floor between your hands (see step 4). Breathe in three times. On the last breath out ...

8 Continue to reverse the sequence of movements and holds in steps 3 and 2, until you are back to position 1. Finish with three deep inhalations, then relax.

more strenuous activities

Rated as the best activity for any level of fitness, walking is a brilliant aerobic exercise that burns fat and lifts the spirits. It costs nothing, does not involve learning any new skill, and benefits every one of us. In time, as you get stronger, you can embark on other forms of aerobic activity as well. Arrange for someone to look after your baby for a couple of hours while you go swimming, rowing, or cycling—but don't overdo it.

THE BENEFITS OF AEROBIC EXERCISE

New research confirms the belief that regular, moderate exercise—moving at a steady pace without becoming breathless for a period of 20 minutes—maximizes the body's aerobic potential to burn fat and boosts the metabolic rate. It also helps to eliminate toxins through the breath and skin, while encouraging the digestive system to work more efficiently.

HOW TO DO THE WALK

□ Whether your favored pace is brisk or slow, if you are out of practice you don't want to overdo things, so give your hamstrings a good stretch before you go walking. Stand with one leg in front of the other, with the knee of the front leg bent, and support yourself with your hands on the front thigh. Keep your back straight and feel the stretch in your straight, rear leg. Repeat twice, then do the same with the other leg.
□ Choose a good route that is not too isolated. Walk in daylight, ideally with a companion.
□ Walk at a brisk but easy pace—slightly faster than usual—for about 5 minutes to get your heart rate and muscles going. Then walk fast for 3 minutes, breathing regularly. Then slow down your walk to a brisk pace for 3 minutes. Repeat the two 3-minute sequences. Finish by walking at an easy pace for the final 3 minutes to cool down. This adds up to a full 20-minute regime.
□ The right choice of stroller is essential when it comes to walking at a fast pace. Its handles need to be at the right level and should not make you stoop as you walk.

Good posture prevents all manner of strains, aches, and pains. It also instantly improves the way you look. If you check that your posture is good at all times—not just while exercising—every movement you make will become a way of toning and strengthening your body.
□ Carry a pedometer to measure how much ground you cover each time you walk, and aim to build up the distance gradually. It can be a great motivator.

WALK TALL

□ Keep your back straight and head held high as you walk. Keeping your shoulders relaxed will help to open out your chest for better, deeper breathing.
□ Walk heel to toe, pushing off with the ball of your rear foot as you bring your other leg forward.
□ Breathe deeply but calmly, with regular inhalations through the nose and regular exhalations through the mouth. If your breathing becomes too fast, slow down— you are working too hard.
□ If you are walking with your baby in a stroller, keep your elbows bent, hands on the stroller at right angles to the handle. If you are carrying your baby in a sling, move your arms while maintaining right angles at the elbows, using your whole body as you walk.
□ Hold in your tummy while you walk. This will help you to maintain good posture, strengthen your back and abdomen, and streamline your figure more quickly.
□ Keep your steps short and quick to give your buttocks more work to do. Squeeze your buttocks as you walk to help strengthen the lower back.

Skipping may be to challenging for you in the first six weeks, but it is one of the best aerobic exercises if you are unable to leave the house. Wonderful for toning buttocks, thighs, and whittling down that waist, it's an all-round cardiovascular workout. Stand up straight, pull your navel in toward your spine, and breathe evenly throughout. At the start, aim to alternate 2 minutes of skipping with 1 minute of mini steps on the spot. Keep your body moving for as long as you can without actually stopping. Try to continue for 20 minutes, but only at a pace that you can happily manage. This is an enjoyable exercise to do with older children.

Swimming builds strength and stamina and, since your body is suspended in water, does not place extra strain on delicate muscles. Try alternating breaststroke, which is great for toning upper arms, with backstroke, which tightens the abdominal muscles and tones arms and legs, for a total body workout. (You can take your baby into the pool after three or four months.)

Cycling boosts stamina and tones the lower body. If possible, stick to open spaces where you don't have to interrupt the flow of your cycling (inner-city cycling burns fewer calories). Remember your posture, and don't slouch. Ideally, the feet should be almost straight when they reach the pedals. (You can attach a baby seat after three or four months.)

DON'T STOP... EVEN WHEN YOU CAN'T GET OUT

activity	calories burned
housework	burns off 35 calories in 20 minutes
kissing	burns off 40 calories in 20 minutes
gardening	burns off 90 calories in 20 minutes
dancing	burns off 80 calories in 20 minutes
playing in the park	burns off 75 calories in 20 minutes

MORE STRENUOUS ACTIVITIES

workout: the early weeks

Some time between six and 12 weeks after the birth, most new mothers start to feel a little more in control—as indeed, their babies become slightly easier to control. If you have been exercising up until now, you can now increase the pace and add a little more intensive tummy and thigh work. If you haven't, begin at the beginning, and take it easy.

OBLIQUE SIT-UPS

This exercise tones the abdominal muscles and waist. If you feel any strain in your back, neck, or shoulders, stop.

1 Lie on your back with your knees raised and your feet flat on the floor. Place a cushion or a rolled-up towel between your knees. Place your hands lightly behind your head, with shoulders and neck relaxed.

2 Breathe in. As you breathe out, pull your navel in toward your spine, tighten your buttocks, and curl up, bringing the right shoulder up in the direction of the left knee. They don't need to touch—so don't over-exert yourself. Smaller intense movements are much more effective at toning tiny essential muscle groups, and will quickly lead to a firmer, leaner silhouette. Repeat with the opposite shoulder and knee.

3 Breathe in and lower your legs to the floor. Repeat five times each side.

BUTTOCK SQUEEZE

As well as toning the lower abdominals and buttocks, this exercise is also good for toning the pelvic floor. Strengthening those muscles protects the back, which is still under great strain. Remember to keep your neck and shoulders completely relaxed.

1 Lie face down on the floor with a cushion under your stomach and a smaller one (a folded hand towel will do) between your thighs. Rest your head with your face turned to one side for comfort.

2 Breathe in. As you breathe out, draw your navel in toward your spine, and at the same time squeeze the cushion between your thighs using the muscles at the base of the buttocks and the inner thighs. Hold for a count of five (which you can increase to ten with time and practice) and release.

3 Repeat five times, keeping relaxed throughout.

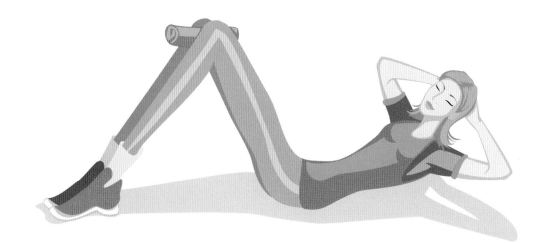

90

CUSHION SQUEEZE

When performed correctly, this exercise is excellent for toning the inner thighs and buttocks, as well as the pelvic floor. The firmer the cushion, the harder it will be.

1 Lie on your back with your knees raised and your feet flat on the floor. Place a cushion (or two) between your knees and keep your arms flat by your sides, palms facing down. Relax your neck and shoulders, and breathe in, pulling up your pelvic-floor muscles.

2 As you breathe out, pull your navel in toward your spine and squeeze the pillow with your knees, tensing your inner thighs. Make sure your back is pressed into the floor, so that only your knees are moving.

3 Breathe in to release the cushion. Repeat ten times.

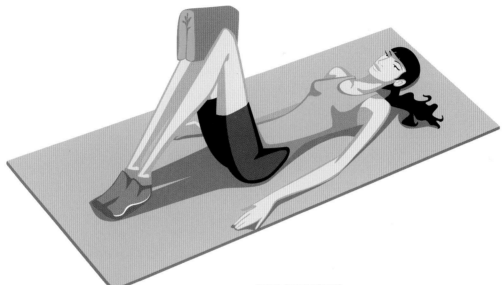

BOTTOM TONER

The stronger you get, the bigger "step" you can make with the cheeks of your bottom in this exercise.

1 Sit upright on the floor with a long straight back. Pull your navel toward your spine, and keep your neck and shoulders relaxed. Stretch your legs out in front of you, feeling the stretch through to your toes. Stretch your arms out in front of you at shoulder height.

2 Moving from your hips, but keeping your back straight, "walk" the right leg forward so that the right foot is in front of the left. Now "walk" the left leg in front of the right. Continue forward for ten steps, then move backward for another ten.

3 If you have any discomfort between your legs or in the perineal area after doing this exercise, wait for another week or two before doing it again.

SIDE STRETCHES

Lift your legs only as high as they can naturally go without tensing the upper body and curving the back.

1 Lie on your side on a mat with your back against a wall, legs stretched out and in line with your back.

2 Stretch out your lower arm on the floor, with your head resting on it, and your upper arm on the floor in front of your chest supporting you lightly. Your face, shoulders, hips, and knees should all face directly forward, without tilting.

3 Breathe in. As you breathe out, pull in your navel toward your spine, flex your feet, and lift them together 2–3 inches (5–8 cm) off the floor. Make sure you stretch away from your body with the heels, rather than lifting the legs high up. Keep your entire body against the wall as you stretch. Hold for a count of five.

4 Breathe in and lower your legs. Repeat ten times in total, making sure there is no tension in your body.

workout: from week 12

After your baby is 12 weeks old, you may feel as if you are getting back to normal, and most exercises you choose to do now will be considered safe. Keep active, stay happy.

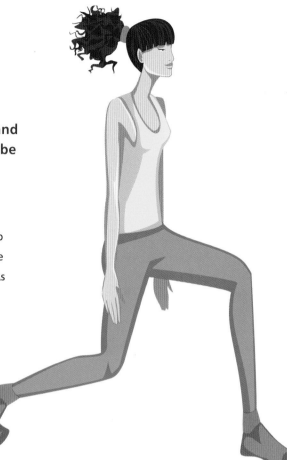

LUNGES

Stand up straight with your feet pointing forward. Step back with each leg alternately and touch the back knee to the floor before returning to the starting position. As you step back, make sure you don't turn out the front foot. You will feel the stretch in your thighs. Do ten lunges, rest, then do ten more.

LEG CURLS

Stand facing a wall. You can rest your hand on the wall for support, but stand up straight—don't lean. Bend one leg so that the foot touches your buttocks, then extend it back straight behind you, with the foot flexed. Hold for a count of three. You should feel this stretch in the hamstring and the back of the thigh. Repeat with the other leg. Do ten leg curls, then rest before doing ten more.

TOE TAPS

Stand up straight and tap one foot at a time, lifting your toes only. Do the taps as quickly as you can. You should feel the stretch in your shin. Repeat ten times with each foot.

INNER AND OUTER THIGH STRETCH

Lie on your back with your legs together stretched out in front of you. Raise them from the floor to an angle of 90 degrees to the rest of your body. Open your legs as far as you can (it does not have to be wide), feeling the stretch in your inner thighs. Close your legs and lower them to the floor. Keep your back pressed into the floor and your shoulders relaxed. Repeat ten times.

PELVIC ROCK

Lie on your back with your feet together, flat on the floor and knees slightly bent. Place a hand under the hollow of your back. Using your abdominal muscles, press your spine against the floor until your back is flat. Relax and repeat ten times.

FULL SQUATS

Keeping your back straight and legs apart, toes pointing forward, squat down as low as feels comfortable, holding onto a chair if you need physical support. Distribute your weight evenly between heels and toes. Hold for a count of three. For a stronger stretch, press your elbows against your inner thighs. Do this ten times.

HALF SQUATS

Place your right foot in front of your left. Point your right knee slightly outward and slowly bend both knees. Keep your bottom tucked in and back straight. Stand up slowly, then repeat with the other leg in front. Do this ten times with each leg.

CRUNCHES

Lie on your back, bend your knees, and rest your arms on your abdomen. Lift your head and shoulders enough to clear the floor using your abdominal muscles. Try not to use your neck or head to help you to lift. Repeat ten times.

THE HUNDRED

This exercise puts quite a strain on the abdominal muscles, so don't try it before you feel ready. If you sense any tension in the neck and shoulders, or any strain in your back, stop immediately and rest.

Lie on your back and draw up your knees so your thighs form a right angle with your chest, keeping them parallel and the feet pointed forward. Stretch out your arms, with pointed fingers, just a few inches from your sides.

Breathe in. As you breathe out, draw the navel in toward the spine, lift your head to look straight toward your thighs, and lift your arms a few inches off the floor. Tap your hands on the floor five times.

Repeat 20 times in total—making a total of 100 taps on the floor.

feel-good factors

Soft and snuggly, dreamily scented, heaven and home in one—that is how your new baby sees you. So how do you see yourself? When new parental responsibilities may seem overwhelming, it is time to focus on the wonderful adventure that is life—and it is time for you, too, to start thinking great things about yourself.

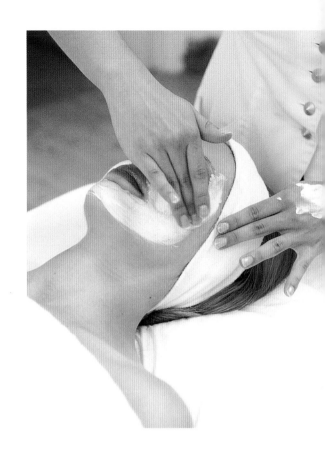

still time for you

In the weeks and months after having a baby, it is all too easy to lose sight of your own needs. But you are the best role model for your child, so it makes sense that you should be happy and contented—not only for your own sake but also for that of your new "family."

PAMPER YOURSELF

This chapter is all about you, the new mother—about how to look and feel as fabulous as you possibly can, at a time when it is tempting to "let yourself go" because there is someone apparently more important to look after. If you get into this frame of mind, you may soon find yourself at the bottom of a big heap of things to do, with the consequence that self-esteem plummets, health declines, and depression sets in. In most cases, all

this could be avoided with a little more self-love, and the easiest way to express self-love is by pampering yourself. Aim to incorporate a few physical treats that remind you that you matter—a great deal. Don't attempt things that take too long—otherwise, they will be impossible to fit into your ever-decreasing time. Think of the ideas on the next few pages as "mommy feels better" rituals that will give you prettier painted toes, softer, naturally scented skin, brighter eyes, and

"We've all lost that self-nurturing principle, and we need to get it back again. There's no doubt that it helps seal the future bond between mother and baby, too."

NOELLA GABRIEL

glossier hair. Your body won't be looking like it did nine months ago for quite some time yet, but these rituals will help to make the most of those parts of your body that are always on show.

COMMUNICATE YOUR FEELINGS

Taking good care of yourself also reminds your equally vulnerable partner that you still have your self-esteem. He may notice mood swings and emotional outbursts, but if he sees you lavishing extra attention on yourself, it will lessen any worries that he has but finds hard to express. It suggests that you are coping and feeling more in control—but do talk about your feelings and ask for help even if you don't feel overwhelmed. If you are aware of a complete lack of interest in the way you look, consider whether you may be suffering from some degree of postpartum depression or "baby blues."

Discuss your feelings with loved ones. You matter most right now. Other people can look after your baby. You alone can really look after yourself.

IT'S HARDER THAN YOU THINK

If you looked after yourself and nurtured yourself as well as your baby in those valuable nine months, then you should be all the more geared up to looking after yourself now, but it can be harder than you think. Just as you have put your newborn down to sleep, and the bath has finished running and you have prepared everything for a relaxing soak, the baby wakes up. But now, more than ever, is the time to remember to treat yourself from top to toe. At a time when most of us feel apprehensive about the way our body has changed, a little pampering helps to relax, soften, and nurture both body and mind. Think of it as the first step to catching a few peaceful moments to yourself. Time to help you focus on yourself rather than your baby.

To make more time for myself, I started having a few salon treatments when I could seize a couple of hours of freedom. The babies often came along, too. Facials, body massages, manicures, pedicures, and blow-drys—every little bit makes you feel more cared for.

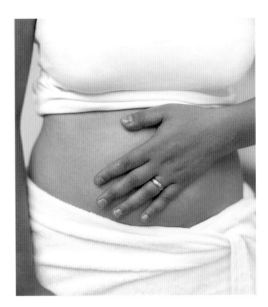

"A dab of neroli essential oil worn between the breasts of a nursing mother can create perfect harmony and happiness for a baby girl. It is like a dozens hugs and happiness rolled into one—and, even into adulthood, the scent may be very powerful and evocative. Choose lemon oil for a baby boy."

NATALIE, FRENCH AROMATHERAPIST

aromatherapy after birth

The healing and soothing effects of aromatherapy can support you both physically and emotionally after you have given birth, and can make this special time a truly enjoyable experience.

HEALING OILS

Jojoba carrier oil massaged into the abdomen during pregnancy and afterward will help keep your skin hydrated and consequently more elastic, reducing the likelihood of stretch marks. This carrier oil—a base oil to which pure essential oils are added in aromatherapy— has anti-inflammatory properties and can be effective in helping to relieve dry, itching skin or eczema which can flare up as hormone levels fluctuate.

Following the birth, essential oils can be particularly effective in treating perineal tears from a difficult delivery. Some midwives may prescribe oils as poultices to help to reduce swelling, while others may suggest adding oils such as lavender (my favorite), geranium, or tea tree to your bath water. Cypress is particularly recommended for bruising and prolonged bleeding as a poultice or in a massage base because of its astringent

action on small blood capillaries. It is also said to be hormonelike, so you might like to add 4 or 5 drops daily your bath to help rebalance the reproductive system after the trauma of childbirth.

The period of recovery after the birth is a time when the body is much more vulnerable to infection and other health problems than usual, so use some of the cleansing aromatherapy oils such as tea tree and lavender to infuse the air and keep germs at bay.

EMOTIONAL BALANCE

Essential oils can ease pain and help to keep emotions well balanced any time of the day. And a scented room is the perfect welcoming environment for a new baby. If you always use the same fragrance, it will become your signature scent—the scent that your baby associates with rest and peace, love and home.

DIFFUSERS

To create a calming, restful environment for my babies when they were small, I used to diffuse 2 drops of lovely geranium essential oil, or 1 drop each of lavender and geranium together, in an electric air diffuser.

Gentler still, place a bowl of warm water containing the same essential oils to diffuse the relaxing aroma around the nursery. Make sure that it is out of reach of small hands or older siblings.

MASSAGE

For a scented massage oil, dilute jasmine, clary sage, lavender or frankincense in a base oil using no more than 2 drops of essential oil per teaspoon of carrier oil. Jasmine and clary sage have traditionally been used in labor to help contractions and to ease muscular pain, and in the postpartum period can help reduce cramps; lavender is both relaxing and invigorating, so use it to balance your emotions at any time. Frankincense is great for creating a sense of calm and is lovely to inhale while you practice deep-breathing rituals.

BOOSTING CIRCULATION

You can massage oils and salts into damp skin for an invigorating body scrub. Stand under the shower for a minute to make sure your whole body is wet, then step out from under the water and grab a handful of salt mixed with an ounce of oil (jojoba, wheatgerm, and almond are beneficial to the skin). For a delicious scent, add 2 drops of orange, lemon, neroli, or patchouli oil.

Starting from the feet, massage the mixture well into your skin. Concentrate on the soles of your feet to help stimulate the body, using circular movements with your whole hand. Move up the legs and the rest of your body, paying particular attention to areas of the body that suffer from a sluggish system such as the thighs, bottom, and backs of arms. Skin here will always appear dimpled or bumpy, but a well-balanced diet and regular care will improve its appearance. Finish by washing off the salt and oils.

USING OILS TO SUIT YOURSELF

Decide which way you can most benefit from the therapeutic effects of essential oils. For tension and stress, I suggest bathing or massaging in the oils or diffusing their aroma while you practice a little deep breathing for relaxation. For physical complaints such as abdominal pains or cramps, soak for about 20 minutes in a bath containing your chosen blend.

Mommy soother

3 drops geranium oil

2 drops neroli oil

1 drop chamomile oil

Combine these three relaxing and fortifying antistress oils together in about 2 ounces of a vegetable carrier oil such as jojoba, sesame or almond oil. Enjoy the mixture in the bath or massaged around your temples, the nape of your neck, and your shoulders. Diffuse the undiluted oils in a diffuser or burner or in a bowl of warm water.

Postpartum lift

2 drops mandarin oil

2 drops lavender oil

2 drops geranium oil

These three refreshing, balancing, and toning oils help improve circulation and energize the system, while encouraging the body to reharmonize after the huge emotional and physical upheaval of childbirth. Inhale the mixture or use it in the bath or as a massage oil.

Tummy smoother

3 drops mandarin oil

3 drops lavender oil

Mandarin and lavender oils, diluted in 2 ounces of carrier oil, are both good at combating stretch marks, but to see the blend's true effect you need really to have used it throughout pregnancy. If you massage it into your skin morning and night from the day of the birth, it will undoubtedly keep the skin smoother and softer and make it better able to spring back into shape.

sometimes you have to say,
quite simply, **"it's my time"**

the luxury of bathing

When chores and responsibilities threaten to overwhelm you, learn to detach yourself from it all for half an hour's peace, and escape to the sanctity of your bathroom. Taking a bath, and enjoying all the ritualistic pleasures that go with it, is one of the greatest antistress agents we have in the home.

WATER THERAPY

Immediately after the birth of our first child, the first thing my husband, Jim, did for me, even while we were still in the labor ward, was to run a warm bath and add 8 drops of pure lavender essential oil. As he cooed over his lovely little babe, I soaked away—and this serene yet euphoric moment is clearly etched in our minds even today. Plus, I was lucky enough to have only one tiny tear as a result of the birth, and thanks to the lavender it had healed completely within four days.

The therapeutic effect on the new mother of bathing and showering cannot be underestimated. To get the most out of those precious few minutes alone in the bathroom, set the scene by playing relaxing music and lighting a mood-enhancing scented candle to help you to unwind. Then give yourself a soothing rub on your neck and shoulders.

Enjoy the aroma of the essential oils that you may have enjoyed in pregnancy, by adding, for example, 3 drops of mandarin and 2 drops of neroli essential oil to the water for a pretty floral bath. Both are also good for the skin and may help to counteract stretch marks, too. Sprinkle the oil onto the water's surface, then mix well just before getting in. Alternatively, pre-blend the oils in 2 teaspoons of a carrier oil or milk, to help it disperse better in the bath. Soak for 20 minutes. Do not use soap because it makes sensitive nipples sore and also ruins the chemical composition of the oils. The calming benefits of tangerine leaf and Roman or Egyptian chamomile essential oils travel through your pores and stimulate your olfactory senses to lull your body and mind into peaceful sleep. Swirl your chosen oil under warm running water.

Lie back and imagine the waves gently lapping around your shoulders. Visualization is the art of relaxation through mental imagery, but it can help you feel energized when you need it, too.

Add 2 drops of lavender and 3 drops of grapefruit essential oil for an herby, zesty bath in the morning or whenever you need a pick-me-up during the day.

HAVING A BATH WITH YOUR BABY

If you want to share a bath with your baby from time to time, buy a non-slip mat for greater safety when getting in or out of the tub. Keep two clean towels at hand (use a separate one from your baby) for when you step out—it's advisable to wrap up babies immediately since they cannot move enough to generate enough body temperature to keep themselves warm.

Before getting into a bath with your baby, make sure that the water is comfortably warm, and not hot: babies are unable to control their own temperature. Have a bottle of oil ready to massage yourself and your baby (see pages 32–33 for massage tips). Or make a pot of chamomile tea and add to your bathwater for a soothing and cooling soak for you both.

From the early days, there are many things you can do to feel at ease in your new role. Tactics as simple as running cold water over your wrists—to cool down the whole body—or sleeping in crisp cotton sheets can put you in a more positive frame of mind and boost your morale.

TEN WAYS TO... *find comfort*

I Wear loose floaty clothing (preferably dresses) that won't constrict you around the middle or between your legs, and open front shirts and loose T-shirts for "easy access" breastfeeding.

2 An icy-cool, damp cloth on the nape of the neck brings down your entire body temperature and keeps you feeling fresh—your body temperature may remain slightly raised for a short time after the birth.

3 Leaking breasts may be a genuine problem, especially at night. Few breast pads are absorbent enough, so, if you have too much milk, you may wake up drenched. While feeding my first baby, I cut up a disposable diaper and used each half as a breast pad at night—it worked. I don't understand why diaper technology has rarely been applied to breast pads.

4 Drinking peppermint tea cools down your body and promotes efficient digestion. If you are breastfeeding, it may be good for your baby's digestion too, since the benefits will be passed on through your breast milk. Other favored herbal teas include fennel, chamomile, and nettle.

5 Lie face down on your tummy at night for an hour or two if you find it comfortable. In the 1960s maternity nurses used to make all new mothers do this to help to flatten the abdomen and reduce the size of the uterus as quickly as possible. Worth a try!

6 An easy-to-wear beauty accessory is a tan, and the safest one is from a bottle. If your legs look slightly golden, you won't feel the need to wear hose, which can feel constricting around the pelvic area after the birth. But do wear those old maternity tights for extra support while your abdominal area regains its shape.

7 Drink plenty of water to help hydrate your body, boost your milk supply, and regulate your body temperature more efficiently.

8 Carry a facial spray around with you when you are traveling by car or public transportation. Add a few favorite essential oils such as 2 drops each of geranium, lavender, and chamomile to a small spray bottle containing spring water and spritz throughout the day. This blend smells divine and doubles as a natural relaxing fragrance when your nose gets too sensitive to the fragrance you usually wear—as well as disguising the smell of regurgitated baby milk in an emergency. A quick spritz of a refreshing spray will also cool down legs and feet.

9 For many new mothers, chamomile balm or cream is invaluable as a treatment for both sore nipples and diaper rash. Decant into a small jar for easy transportation.

IO Press on Ayurvedic vital points on the body (called *marmas*) that promote calm: the center of the forehead and the back of the neck. Then spritz a little geranium and lavender oil, blended in some water, around your neck and shoulders, and breathe in deeply.

taking care of number one

Lavish attention on certain parts of your body to help you feel more cared for. There is nothing very attractive about leaking breasts, red stretch marks, and dry itchy skin, and at some moments you may feel less than in control of your body. But give yourself time—time to cope, time to settle, time to adapt to being a mother—before you start trying to reclaim physical equilibrium.

SOOTHING SORE NIPPLES

If your nipples become cracked or sore, feed your baby for shorter periods, but more often. Breast milk is a natural healer, and midwives recommend applying it as a remedy for sore, cracked nipples. (It is also a great remedy for the "sticky eye" condition that many babies develop.) Specialized creams and tinctures such as Hyper Cal, Kamillosan, and Calendula are very effective at soothing and healing cracked nipples. Use them sparingly between feeds over a period of 2 to 3 days.

Sore nipples can persist for a couple of weeks, but the condition will resolve itself. Expressing milk with a breast pump stimulates the nipples, and although it will increase the amount of breast milk you produce, it may accustom the nipples to being pulled.

STRETCH MARKS

If you have stretch marks, console yourself with the fact that they're hereditary and were almost inevitable. The good news is that those red lines gradually fade during the six months after birth, becoming silvery and far less noticeable, especially in people with fair skin. According to skincare experts, if you did not moisturize and oil your skin before you were four months' pregnant, it was by then already too late to prevent stretch marks.

If you are worried about stretch marks, consider whether you should nurture a more positive self-image. I saw the flame-shaped marks rising around my tummy as my "birth" marks. I decided to love my marks because they reflected what I'd been through; they immediately became a positive thing—and since then, I've never worried one bit about them.

SKIN CHANGES

During pregnancy, previous skin blemishes and skin problems such as acne or excessive oiliness are reversed or reduced, sometimes for good. But the hormonal upheaval that follows childbirth can also wreak havoc on your skin, causing flare-ups of dry skin conditions such as psoriasis, eczema, acne, and dermatitis, plus an irreversible increase in the size and number of skin moles and an inclination toward skin tags.

Your skin is at its most sensitive during the period immediately after the birth, so allow a while to let everything calm down, and be prepared to adapt your skin care regime for the next few months.

TOWEL TONIC

When you feel tired or anxious, undress and towel yourself all over as hard as you can with a clean, rough towel. Include the top of your head, behind your ears, ankles, feet, lips, and nose. Then take a handful of fresh basil or sage leaves and step into a hot shower. Stroke the herbs all over your body as you shower for 1 minute. Then shower in warm for 5 minutes. Towel dry vigorously again to finish.

where's the bloom?

After pregnancy, skin changes in much the same way as it does during puberty and menopause. These are all times of dramatic fluctuation in the body's level of estrogen, the hormone that gives skin its suppleness, moisture, and smoothness.

LOOKING AFTER YOUR FACE

Make your skincare regime as simple as possible. Switch your cleanser to an all-skin-types pure cleanser such as Aqueous Cream BP, which you can comfortably use on normal skin and problem skin alike. Plus, since Aqueous Cream has a moisturizing effect, you will have less need to use any occlusive creams on top; instead, allow your skin to find its own balance.

□ **If your skin feels drier,** look for creamier cleansers and face masks that you can gently wipe off with a tissue or soft muslin cloth, and cream moisturizers that will act as a barrier, retaining moisture in the skin and protecting it from the drying effect of the sun.

□ **If your skin feels oilier,** look for oil-based cleansers that help to dissolve oil and dirt from pores, clay-based masks to help draw out any further impurites, a T-zone control product to minimize shine, and a light oil-free moisturizer to apply only to areas of dry patches such as on the cheeks. If you have acne, avoid masks. Go for the "less is more" approach, and try body rebalancing therapies such as acupuncture and homeopathy. A facial steam using 3 drops of lavender or tea-tree oil dispersed in a bowl of hot water, will gently cleanse, soothe, and heal vulnerable skin.

□ **If your skin looks patchy,** those post-pregnancy hormones are the culprits. These increase the melanin production in the skin, leaving a darker pigmented area, usually over the face and cheeks, resulting in a patchy-looking condition called chloasma. Middle-toned and olive skins are more susceptible, but it usually fades after the birth. The more that your skin has been (and continues to be) exposed to the sun, the more stubborn and persistent these patches tend to be. And subsequent sun exposure will usually bring them out again (even though you aren't pregnant), so you will need to protect your skin from daily UV exposure with a product with a sun protection factor of 15 or higher.

BODY CHANGES

Where there was once a stretched-out bump, there is now a large area of slack skin that feels sloshy for the first week or two. I was shocked by this and found it hard to believe that the skin would shrink back. But, though many of us, after first or later pregnancies, may complain of the roll of flesh that does not appear to be affected by exercise, it is amazing how much your body recovers after childbirth.

□ Changes in skin pigmentation that took place in pregnancy on the nipples and the areola start to fade.

□ The dark vertical line (the linea nigra) down the center of the tummy soon disappears.

□ The belly button quickly looks more like it used to.

□ As your body gets back to normal, you will feel the uterine contractions and abdominal cramps begin to pass with each passing day. Your first period (which usually occurs around four to six months after the birth, or longer if you are breastfeeding) may feel like strong cramping pains. When this happened to me, I massaged in plenty of Clarins Relax Body Treatment Oil (rich in lavender and geranium), and the pains soon passed.

□ Your skin is very sensitive after the birth (often even more so than your baby's), so avoid using any new detergents. Wash and dry your body frequently and, if you like, use talcum powder to keep the skin dry. Soothe the skin with cooling calendula lotion and wear loose cotton clothing in warm weather.

SKIN-SAVING TIPS

□ Apply a high-protection sunscreen at least half an hour before exposing your body to the sun.

□ Keep your baby out of the sun until the age of six months, and even after that limit sun exposure. Use a minimum of a SPF25 sunscreen on any exposed skin.

□ Eat your greens—and your reds. The more color in your diet, the larger quantity of essential vitamins and skin-regenerating antioxidants you will benefit from.

□ Drink filtered or bottled water and consume organic produce whenever possible to cut down on the ever-increasing number of toxins and chemicals in our bodies—which place an immediate and long-term stress on our physical equilibrium.

"During pregnancy you will probably spend 90 percent of your time preparing for the birth and 10 percent preparing for after the birth. Once the baby had arrived, I wished I'd spent 10 percent preparing for the birth itself, and 90 percent getting ready for the rest of my life."

NATALIE, MOTHER OF LUCAS AND MANON

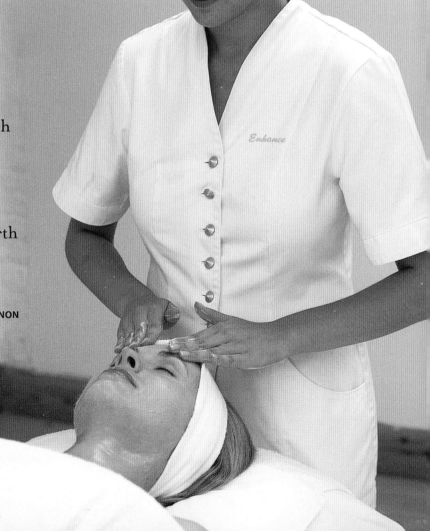

what's happened to my hair?

Well over half of new mothers notice some degree of hair loss, some even losing fistfuls of hair, usually three to four months after a baby is born (although breastfeeding may delay this). The good news is that hair loss is perfectly normal—and virtually always temporary.

WHY DOES IT HAPPEN?

During pregnancy, the growing phase of the hair cycle is extended, so that each hair stays in place for longer and looks—and is—thicker. But after the birth, the resting phase, which has been delayed, kicks in all at once, and suddenly those months of missed hair shedding happen all at once. Since no new hairs have been growing behind the old hairs, suddenly you have a lot less hair.

WHAT CAN YOU DO ABOUT IT?

No treatment is necessary because the problem will resolve itself over the next six to nine months. The best way to make sure your hair grows back beautifully is to eat a diet rich in B vitamins, zinc, iron, selenium, and amino acids. "The most common mistake," says leading trichologist Glen Lyons, "is for new moms to start dieting in an attempt to regain their figure as fast as possible." The message is: if you feed yourself properly, your hair will look after itself.

Once new hairs start to grow back, you may find that they stick up in all directions—and a number of women experience a "fringe" of baby hair. Having new hair growing through is a good reason to choose a shorter style. That way, you can blend the hairs into a more layered look so they don't appear so out of place.

TIPS FOR HEALTHY HAIR

☐ Frequent washing cleanses the scalp and encourages healthier, shinier hair. Wash your hair every day or every other day with a mild shampoo. Always choose a shampoo suitable for the condition of your scalp and a conditioner suitable for the condition of your hair.

☐ Minimize blow drying. Hair that is left to air-dry, using the bare minimum of styling products, will be in better condition and suffer less from split ends and breakage.

☐ Use a comb instead of a brush. Gently comb the hair while curling the ends upward to avoid overstretching, which will cause it to break, especially while wet.

☐ Eat regularly. Too long a gap between meals—more than four hours—starves individual hair follicles of vital nutrients, resulting in weaker hair with uneven cuticles.

☐ Minimize chemical processing. Coloring and perming alter the natural structure of hair and is ultimately drying and damaging. Try to have less done to your hair and indulge in intensive conditioning treatments.

☐ Protect your hair from weathering. Hair is exposed on a daily basis to the effects of sun, wind, pollution, chlorinated water, and sea water—all of which roughen the surface texture and reduce shine and luster. At the very least, wear a hat in extremes of weather (sun, rain, wind) and when swimming in a pool.

lighter, lovelier legs

It is not surprising that we experience a lot of discomfort in our legs and feet during pregnancy, while carrying so much extra weight. Although problems may persist after the birth, you now have a chance to reach your legs again and pamper them all over.

PROBLEMS AFFECTING THE LEGS

Cramps, swelling, spider veins, varicose veins—let's face it, after nine months of carrying around between 15 and 60 pounds (7 and 27 kg) of additional weight, any or all of these conditions could affect your legs.

Swelling of the legs and ankles (called edema) is caused by an increase in fluid retention in the body, especially in the lower limbs. It is common to find that your legs and ankles are still swollen after the birth—especially if you had an epidural. Avoid standing for

long periods, and rest with your feet raised. It may help to wear maternity support tights. Avoid wearing pop socks, tight socks, or tight shoes. Exercise can help to prevent swelling by boosting circulation. Try gentle foot exercises: sit comfortably upright in a chair, stretch one foot out, and gently rotate your ankles and feet to increase circulation. Repeat with the other leg.

Varicose or swollen veins are due to increased venous pressure and the effect of "relaxing" hormones during pregnancy that soften blood vessel walls. Try to take regular exercise and avoid standing for long periods. Cross your legs at the ankles (not the knees), start to watch your weight, and avoid wearing anything that's too tight or constricting.

Effective medical treatments are available to deal with painful or unsightly veins. Varicose veins can be removed (stripped out) by a doctor under anesthetic. In a process called sclerotherapy, red spider veins can be quickly dissolved using a chemical solution that safely collapses these tiny little veins so that the accumulated blood within the vein disappears.

Cellulite affects around 80 percent of women, especially around puberty and pregnancy. So you may notice it more now than ever before. A healthy eating plan that features more fresh fruit and vegetables and fewer sugary snacks will not only give you more energy, but will also reduce the amount of cellulite.

Many new mothers are affected by cramps in the legs, especially at night. The main cause is the change in hormones and chemicals in the muscles that leads to spasms. Learn to stretch your legs before bed, keep them warm, and gently exercise the calf muscles. Avoid pointing the toes since this can trigger cramp; instead learn to flex your foot backward with your heel thrust forward. Massage helps to relieve cramps.

STIMULATE CIRCULATION

Sit or stand with your feet flat on the floor. Lift up your toes and point them toward you, keeping your heels flat on the floor. Lower your toes and with a rolling action lift your heels. Repeat 15–20 times.

Alternatively, give yourself a lymphatic massage, using a little of your favorite lotion, cream, or oil. Start with the soles of your feet, applying gentle pressure to the arch of your foot and between your toes. Then gently stroke your legs upward from the ankle to the knee, finishing with firm pressure behind the knee.

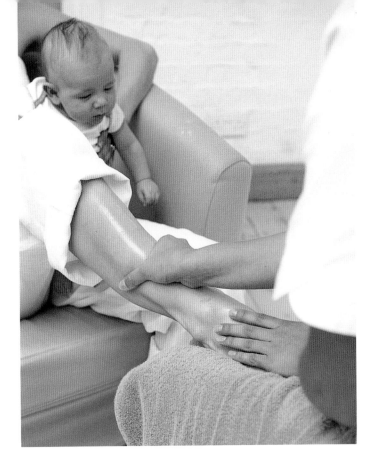

PAMPER YOUR FEET

Your feet have carried you through the whole nine months. For a quick treat, give them a mini-pedicure.

□ Soak feet in warm water for 10 minutes, either in a large bowl or using a gently vibrating foot spa. Add 3 drops of lavender and 2 drops of geranium essential oil to help you relax further.

□ Pat feet dry and buff away hard skin away using a hard pumice stone, or massage in a little exfoliating grains for a couple of minutes, then rinse.

□ Massage in some soothing cream, paying particular attention to the area around the toenails and heels.

□ Allow the cream to be absorbed, then add a light layer of cooling foot gel.

□ If you like wearing polish, wipe your toenails clean of cream, then apply a quick single coat.

□ To avoid smudging the polish, apply a coat of fast-drying top coat and wear a pair of flip-flops or keep your feet bare until the nails are touch dry.

INSTANT REVIVERS

□ When your legs ache, massage them with an oil made from a blend of menthol, peppermint, and cedarwood.

□ Fake tan takes the edge off pasty skin, gives you a natural-looking glow, and makes you feel more radiant even when you are exhausted.

□ Massage plenty of moisturizing cream into dry skin. Apply more cream than usual, lie back on your bed for 5 minutes with your baby next to you, or pad around with no clothes on for a few minutes, to give the lotion time to be absorbed before you get dressed.

don't forget that, although you are a **mommy** to someone, you are **first** and **foremost** still you

turn any **negative** feelings about your body into **positives**;
your tummy, scars, and stretch marks are evidence that
you've been through a **life-changing** experience

make yourself look good ...
to make yourself feel good

Looking good doesn't have to take all night—let alone all day. But going somewhere special is a good excuse to pay yourself some extra attention. It will help you to feel more attractive and more confident about yourself—and to rediscover your old identity.

SIZE ISN'T EVERYTHING

Don't get obsessed about regaining your pre-pregnancy size and shape. It takes time for your body to heal and rebalance in so many ways. We are all individual, and there is no doubt that some women find it easier than others to slim down. Just as breastfeeding helps some women to lose weight naturally, it makes others gain weight because of their need for extra energy foods. Now is the time to feel good about what you have achieved, and to relish the fact that you are a mother.

LOOK GORGEOUS AND GLAMOROUS

□ Choose flattering fashions such as bias-cut skirts and dresses and tops that drape and float around your body rather than clinging to areas that you might prefer to distract attention from. A delicate floaty scarf in elaborate or ornate fabric or a drop-waist style will divert the eye from your waistline. Wear open cardigans to streamline your silhouette. And make the most of that ample cleavage and radiant smile!

□ The simple act of applying lipstick is reckoned by some psychologists to boost a woman's self-esteem tenfold. In turn, making more of an effort with your looks after having a baby—when you are at your most tired—will renew your self-confidence and will ultimately make you appear more sexy and alluring, even when you don't necessarily feel it. Why not change an item of makeup or alter your hairstyle—just do something that makes you feel good about yourself.

□ Add a summery glow. The new generation of fake tans look as good as the real thing and take the edge off pasty skin, especially if you are exposing shoulders and your newly enhanced cleavage. It takes less time than you think. If you want to apply a self-tan product, be sure to exfoliate your skin first, and moisturize your skin for several days leading up to the application to help soften your skin and avoid discoloration.

□ Shimmer and gleam. Dust a little super-fine shimmery golden loose powder or a creamy shimmer lotion over shoulders, collarbone, cheeks, and brows, and that heaving bossom—to make your skin gleam and look all the more alluring.

□ Indulge in sexy underwear. I don't mean tiny weeny items that make you feel even worse about your figure than you may already feel—but a pretty, lacy, all-in-one body suit, for example, that looks sexy but also stretches and supports your diminishing tummy without digging into your skin. It will also give your body a shapelier appearance under clothes.

BREATHE DEEPLY

Practice deep breathing for inner calm and patience as well as healthier-looking skin. Lie down comfortably, horizontally, with your knees raised under a pillow or cushion. Breathe in and out slowly and evenly from the abdomen, not the chest, sighing each breath out, while trying to relax and empty your mind. Continue for five to ten minutes whenever you have a bit of peace.

quick-fix makeover

**Whenever you need a quick wake-up call, and can snatch just
half an hour to yourself, try any one of these skin-brightening
tips and treats to make you look and feel like "you" again.**

A RADIANT NEW YOU

Treat yourself to a facial. Give someone else the chance
to look at your skin now you have had a baby. A skilled
beautician will check oiliness, dryness, and patchiness,
and re-evaluate your skincare regime and pamper your
skin so that you look as radiant as you did when you
were pregnant—even when you don't feel it.

The benefits of a facial last for at least a week: skin
clarity, less obvious pores, smoothness, and better tone
and circulation that belie a general lack of sleep.

OTHER SURVIVAL STRATEGIES

☐ Take time out for a face or eye mask. It is an excellent
way to force yourself to take a well-earned rest, at any
time of the day, and lie still for 10–15 minutes, while
your baby suckles or simply lies peacefully.

☐ Buff up your skin and keep yourself feeling fresh
and lively with a facial exfoliator once or twice a week,
depending on how sensitive your skin is.

☐ Keep some eye cream in the fridge: nothing wakes
up tired, puffy eyes faster first thing in the morning.

RELAX AND ENJOY

Book in for a massage. Get daddy or grandma to look
after your baby guilt-free for a couple of hours, or do
swaps with a friend, every one or two weeks.

Soothe away stress and ease tension around the neck
and shoulders with a lavender-filled pillow. Make your
own from dried lavender buds. Cut a piece of soft close-
weave cloth twice the desired size of your pillow. Stitch
up two edges, fill the open end with dried lavender
buds, then sew up into a pillow.

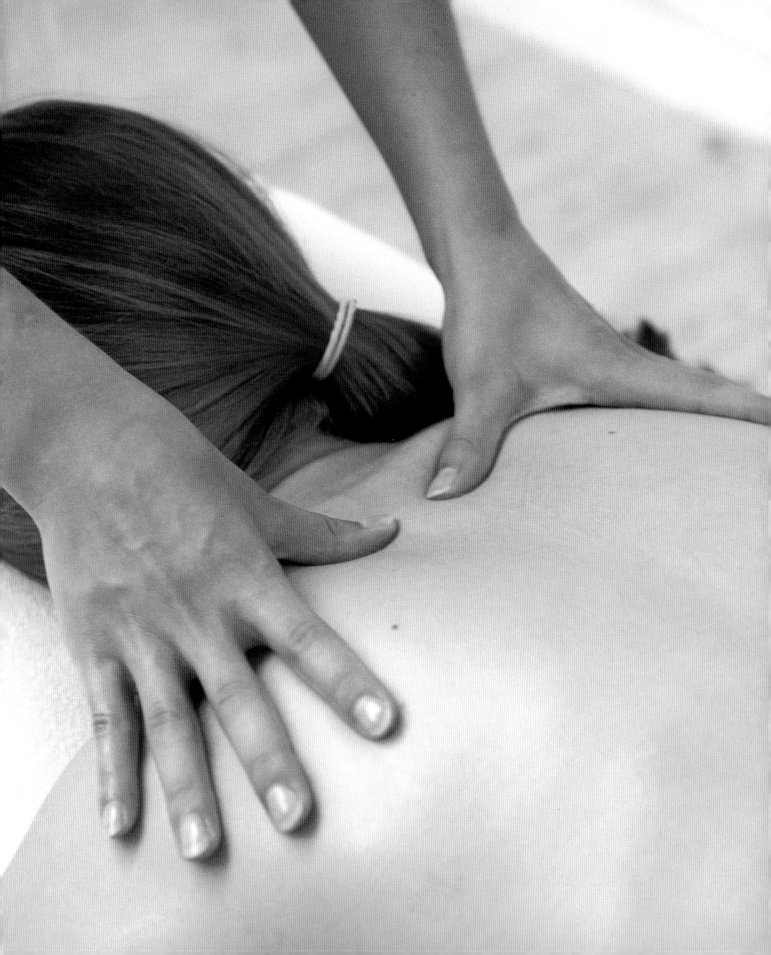

Right now you are probably witnessing the dire consequence of broken nights: tired, puffy, dark eyes. But there are plenty of things you can do to hide the fact that you feel like a walking zombie. Looking less tired is half way to feeling less tired.

TEN WAYS TO... *hide tiredness*

I   For a quick fix, soak and chill two chamomile tea bags (used ones are fine), lie down and place on your closed eyelids for 10 minutes.

2   Lilac is the most "awakening" eye color any woman can wear. It immediately lifts and brightens the eyes. Find under-eye powders and luminous skin creams that have that mother-of-pearl quality about them.

3   If you are waking up with puffy eyes, wrap an ice-cube in a hanky and glide it over your face, from the inside corner of the nose to the ear and down the side of the face to just under the jaw. Repeat on both sides several times. It's a real wake-up call and feels fabulous.

4   Try using an extra pillow in bed and sleep on your back to stop fluid from pooling around the eyes.

5   If you have naturally droopy eyes, dot a tiny amount of concealer or pale shimmer at the outer corners of each eye, where the top lashes meet the bottom, and your eyes will look instantly brighter, wider, more awake.

6 "Palming" is a gentle pressure massage to stop puffiness. With fingers pointing up toward the top of your head, gently press the heels of your hands onto the tops of the cheekbones. Rest palms gently on eyelids so you can feel the heat they generate.

7 To flush toxins out of your system, you need to drink more fluid—ideally water, and most of it in the morning. But, for the purposes of hydration (especially while you are breastfeeding), you can get your daily requirement of up to 10 glasses (80 ounces) of fluid a day from a mix of water, teas, and juice, according to guidelines issued by the National Academy of Sciences.

8 Cover up dark circles. Hold a mirror in front of you, and, keeping your chin lowered, look up into it so you can see clearly where your dark circles need concealing. Pat concealer on the inside corner of the eye only—the darkest bit—and blend lightly.

9 Eyelash curlers curl the lashes upward and "open up" the eye. Straight lashes that point downward may make you look sleepy.

IO Eating more fresh fruit and vegetables will keep you feeling lighter and livelier, and will relieve any constipation that may cause darkness around the eyes.

pampering and beauty rituals

Set aside a couple of hours a week for pampering. Have a manicure, pedicure, massage, body scrub, wax, fake tan, facial—whatever makes you feel good about yourself. Book a treatment session or do it yourself. Concentrate on the essentials —hands, nails, brows, and makeup—and give yourself a top-to-toe makeover with the aim of feeling thoroughly groomed and gorgeous. In preparation for a quick me-time experience at home, lower the lighting, keep it warm, play relaxing music, and make sure you have everything you need on hand.

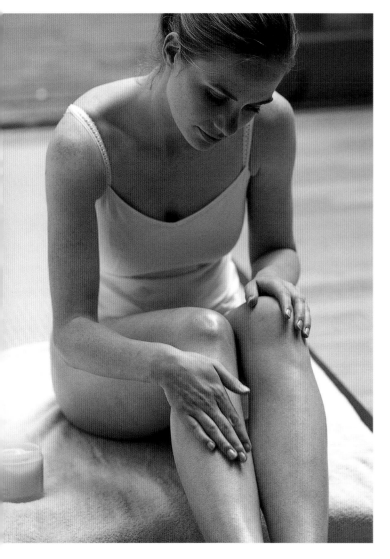

START WITH YOUR FEET

Using a new pumice stone or metal foot file, buff the dry, rough skin on the heels and balls of your feet, paying special attention to any corns and calluses that need smoothing away. Do this before showering or bathing so that you remove hard (not softened) skin.

BUFF YOUR WHOLE BODY

A body scrub is one of the most effective ways to boost the look and feel of your skin in an instant—yet it is a ritual quickly dispensed with when time is short. Exfoliation also encourages the more efficent absorption of creams and potions.

A little sea salt held in the palm of your hand and gently rubbed all over bumpy dry-skin areas is the easiest and cheapest exfoliator. If you add a little oil (such as almond, wheatgerm, or jojoba), the salt will glide over the skin more easily and leave your body with a super-soft gleam that feels baby-soft, too.

SOFTEN AND SMOOTH ALL OVER

Next, massage a lovely natural-scented body cream such as rose or geranium into dry-skin areas that need extra love and attention—heels, toes, ankles, knees, shins, elbows, backs of arms, cuticles, and cleavage. Really work the cream into your skin in small circular massage strokes, stimulating circulation as you rub. One of the best daily rituals you can adopt is to massage a little rich cream into your hands and feet before climbing into bed at night. It will truly transform them.

WRAP UP WARM AND COZY FOR TEN MINUTES

While your skin is absorbing the moisturizer, lie back in peace on a bed, propped up on pillows, and give yourself a spine-tingling, soothing scalp massage.

Close your eyes and relax your neck and shoulders. Gently rub tiny circles along your neck and up to the nape of your neck. Press all along each side of your hairline at intervals of an inch, until you reach the hair's center part. Then place all your fingers and thumbs in your hair and gently massage your scalp with tiny little circular movements, followed by a press on the scalp. Aim to cover the entire scalp area, massaging gently but firmly, and lifting your fingers out of your hair and placing them in again as you go. Do this for three minutes. Next lift your hair upward with your fingers, pulling very gently, and hold for two counts. Repeat several times. Use scalp oil throughout if you prefer, but it will need to be shampooed out afterwards.

PAINT YOUR FINGERS AND TOES

At the first reunion of my prenatal group after we'd had our babies, one mother arrived with fingernails and toenails newly painted bright red. It looked fantastic and made every other mother feel drab by comparison —so the next week we all did the same. Such an indulgence gives just a small psychological lift—but it works. It proves that you're still you and that you still care about you. You may prefer "sugar-baby pink" for the first six to 12 weeks, but the point is that you are giving yourself moments of pampering, however small.

TIRED TO RADIANT IN FIVE EASY STEPS

□ Spritz your face with water or toner to refresh the skin, then gently wipe clean, removing the day's powder and foundation.

□ Apply a little concealer just where you need it, dust over a little loose powder, then place a little rosy blusher to the apple of your cheeks.

□ Freshen up the day's eye makeup with a damp cotton swab, then apply a touch of shimmery eyeshadow to the lids only, blending with your finger.

□ Curl your lashes (it makes a big difference) and apply one coat of thickening mascara.

□ A glossy mouth is very fashionable, easy to apply, and a pretty way to make small or thin lips appear bigger.

you must **nurture** yourself to nurture **another** –

and this is an important time to **fulfill** your own **needs**

conclusion

I love motherhood. I do think it's marvelous. I cherish my children so much. They are my life—and they have made my life more valuable for having had them. With every stage of their development—from birth to toddlerhood and early school years—our relationship continues to grow ever deeper, based on huge amounts of love and respect.

A dear friend of mine, John P., once summed up my relationship with my children. "All mommies love their children," he said. "The difference is you 'like' them, too." He was right. To me, my children really are enjoyable to be with, and I both love and like them. Nurturing positive feelings toward babies and children is a crucial part of motherhood, helping them feel confident, happy, and valued as individuals long before they reach the playground. And I believe that these positive feelings—both yours and theirs—should start from birth. Every hug and kiss, your tone of voice (ideally, calm and reassuring), the scent of your skin when you hold them close to you, each caress of their tiny head and neck—these simple gestures and elements stimulate your baby's senses and develop your baby's ability to love in return.

Whether you have become a mother for the first, third, or fifth time, I hope that you have found this book useful and, above all, supportive, and that it has encouraged you to love and look after yourself more diligently—because in feeling happier about yourself, you will undoubtedly be a happier and better mother. These days, a great deal of discussion takes place about how our parents shaped the person

we are—in good and often not so good respects. Every day, I recognize in my natural responses to my children the responses I learned in one way or another from own parents. Our reactions and behavior are learned from the people who raised us. Awareness of this fact is half the battle in improving our attempts at parenting.

Your children learn their attitudes to self from you. If you put yourself down, the chances are that they will do the same. If you get angry at the smallest thing, guess who will follow suit. If you radiate serenity and contentment whenever possible (OK—that's just the ideal), and show your children that you are happy to have them to love, everyone in the home will benefit.

In my pregnancy book, *Blossoming Beauty*, I linked the idea of a happy baby—even in the womb—with a happy mother. Much that you experience in pregnancy your baby experiences, too. Stress has its effect, just as diet does. The way our behavior affects our children starts earlier than we imagine, so don't leave it until your child has tantrums before wondering why. Learn to manage and cope with yourself and your feelings before you start telling someone else how to behave. Good parenting begins with the parents.

I hope that the first year goes well for you—most of all because babies are tiny for such a short time that it's a shame to wish away those early days. You will not believe the changes that take place—both in you and your baby—during the first year. Please enjoy this time. They are toddlers before you know it. But that's another story . . .

resources

**Academy of
Breastfeeding Medicine**
191 Clarksville Road
Princeton Junction, NJ 08550
877-836-9947
www.bfmed.org
*Breastfeeding education
and support.*

**American Academy
of Pediatrics**
141 Northwest Point Blvd
P.O. Box 927
Elk Grove Village, IL 60009
800-433-9016
www.aap.org
*Health information about
babies and children.*

**American Massage Therapy
Association**
500 Davis Street, Suite 900
Evanston, IL 60201-4695
847-864-0123
www.amtamassage.org
*Help with finding a massage
therapist near you.*

**The Center for
Postpartum Health**
20700 Ventura Blvd, Ste 203
Woodland Hills, CA 91364
818-887-1312
www.postpartumhealth.com
*Looks after the psychological
and emotional needs of the
new mother, with an emphasis
on dealing with depression.*

**Childbirth and Postpartum
Professional Association**
P.O. Box 491448
Lawrenceville, GA 30049
888-MY-CAPPA

www.cappa.net
*International organization that
cares for women before,
during, and after birth through
education and support.*

The Cranial Academy
8202 Clearvista Parkway #9-D
Indianapolis, IN 46256
www.cranialacademy.org
*Help with finding a cranial
osteopath in your area.*

Doulas of North America
P.O. Box 626
Jasper, IN 47547
801-756-7331
www.dona.com
Information on doulas.

FDA Office of Women's Health
Food and Drug Administration
5600 Fishers Lane
Rockville, MD 20857
888-463-6332
www.fda.gov/womens/
*Information on a wide range of
women's health issues.*

4nannies.com Inc.
2 Pidgeon Hill Dr. Suite 550
Potomac Falls, VA 20165
800-810-2611
www.4nannies.com
*Online resource helping parents
find nannies.*

KidsHealth.org
*All-round website for parents
and children, reviewed by
doctors; covers everything from
birth to nutrition. Sponsored
by the Nemours Foundation
Center for Children's Health.*

La Leche League
PO Box 1209
Franklin Park, IL 60131
800-525-3243
www.lalecheleague.org
*Support and information for
breastfeeding mothers, and on
local La Leche League groups
across the country.*

**Midwives Alliance of
North America**
4805 Lawrenceville Hwy
Suite 116-279
Lilburn, GA 30047
888-923-6262
www.mana.org
Information on midwives.

**National Acupuncture and
Oriental Medicine Alliance**
6405 43rd Avenue Ct. NW, Ste B
Gig Harbor, WA 98335
253-851-6896
www.acuall.org
*Information on complementary
and alternative medicine and on
finding a practitioner near you.*

**National Healthy Mothers,
Healthy Babies Coalition**
121 North Washington Street
Suite 300
Alexandria, VA 22314
703-836-6110
www.hmhb.org
*Works to improve health and
safety of mothers and babies.*

**National Women's Health
Information Center**
www.4woman.gov
800-994-WOMAN

*Website and helpline providing
information on many aspects
of women's health, including
postpartum depression.*

**National Women's Health
Resource Center**
157 Broad Street, Suite 315
Red Bank, NJ 07701
877-986-9472
www.healthywomen.org
*Information resource designed
to encourage women to pursue
healthy lifestyles.*

The New Parents Guide
www.thenewparentsguide.com
*Online resource for parenting
information.*

www.breastfeeding.com
*All-purpose breastfeeding
support site; includes a
national directory of lactation
consultants.*

index

author's acknowledgments

Behind every marvelous "working" mother there has to be a marvelous father—or his mother!
Thank you to my Jim and my dear mother-in-law, Sylvia, for supporting me always, in everything.
And of course to my adorable children, Olivia, William, and Phoebe—who constantly remind me
how much I love being a mother. Thank you to my agent, Fiona Lindsay of Limelight Management,
and to all at Ryland Peters & Small, particularly Alison Starling, Henrietta Heald, and Sonya Nathoo.
Thanks to my favorite aromatherapy experts, Noella Gabriel of Elemis and Glenda Taylor of Enata,
and to many colleagues and friends in the beauty and wellbeing industry, including Kate Hudson,
Carri Kilpatrick, Nancy Brady, Liz Earle, and (nearly Uncle) John Prothero. And lastly thank you to
those without whom motherhood would be a lonely old journey, my friends and fellow mothers:
Catherine Everest, Suzanne Wilson, Esther de Vries, Ilona Zurmmond, Liz Scalzo, Gina de Ferrer,
Donna Hilton, Eve Cameron, Diana Collier, Carolyn O'Neill, Carla Franke, and Lara Philpott.

publishers' acknowledgments

The publishers would like to say thank you to all our models, especially
Antonia and Miley, Lynn and Madoc, Lalaine, Poppy and Sam, Louise
and Ralph, Deborah and Charles. Thanks also to beauty therapist
Lauren at Enhance Beauty and Skin Care Centre, 60 Banstead Road,
Carshalton, Surrey SM5 3NL, UK (+ 44-(0)20-8652-6688).

photography credits

Front and back jacket by DAN DUCHARS.

Photography by DAN DUCHARS unless otherwise stated.
Key: a=above, b=below, r=right, l=left, c=center.

© STOCKBYTE 4–5, 7, 13, 16, 19, 25, 30 inset,
35, 55, 73, 94; DAVID MONTGOMERY 15, 20r,
22, 23, 80 background, 102 background, 112
background, 125; POLLY WREFORD 18, 24, 26,
49, 71, 100 Ros Fairman's house in London;
TOM LEIGHTON 30 background; CAROLINE
ARBER 36 background; NICKY DOWEY 42, 48c,
64a; PETER CASSIDY 43l, 59; IAN WALLACE
45, 60, 61c; WILLIAM SHAW 47, 48l, 61l;
MARTIN BRIGDALE 48r; SIMON UPTON 61r;
GUS FILGATE 62; DAVID MUNNS 64b; CHRIS
EVERARD 69, 74; DEBI TRELOAR 81a, 128
Vincent AND Frieda Plasschaert's house in
Brugge, Belgium; DANIEL FARMER 99.